The Power of UN Ideas: Lessons from the First 60 Years

Richard Jolly, Louis Emmerij, and Thomas G. Weiss

A Summary of the Books and Findings from the
United Nations Intellectual History Project

New York, May 2005

Library of Congress Cataloging-in-Publication data
A catalog record has been requested

ISBN 0-976-56550-1

Designed, edited, and produced by Communications Development Incorporated, Washington, DC, with Grundy & Northedge, London

Table of Contents

Abbreviations

CEDAW	Convention on the Elimination of All Forms of Discrimination against Women
CSW	Commission on the Status of Women
ECA	Economic Commission for Africa
ECE	Economic Commission for Europe
ECLA	Economic Commission for Latin America
ECLAC	Economic Commission for Latin America and the Caribbean
ECOSOC	Economic and Social Council
ESCAP	Economic and Social Commission for Asia and the Pacific
ESCWA	Economic Social Commission for West Africa
FDI	foreign direct investment
GNP	gross national product
HDI	human development index
HIPC	heavily indebted poor country
HIV/AIDS	human immunodeficiency virus/acquired immune deficiency syndrome
IDA	International Development Association
ILO	International Labour Organization
IMF	International Monetary Fund
INSTRAW	International Research and Training Institute for the Advancement of Women
MDG	Millennium Development Goal
NGO	nongovernmental organization
OECD	Organisation for Economic Co-operation and Development
SUNFED	Special UN Fund for Economic Development
TNC	transnational corporation

U.K.	United Kingdom
UN	United Nations
UNCTAD	UN Conference on Trade and Development
UNDP	UN Development Programme
UNESCO	UN Educational, Scientific and Cultural Organization
UNICEF	UN Children's Fund
UNIFEM	UN Development Fund for Women
UNIHP	UN Intellectual History Project
UNSO	UN Statistical Office
U.S.	United States
WHO	World Health Organization
WTO	World Trade Organization

UN Contributions to Development Thinking and Practice

Anniversaries are a wonderful moment to take stock and look to the future. On the occasion of the UN's 60th, three crucial documents looking forward are before member states, one from the High-level Panel on Threats, Challenges and Change, a second from the Millennium Project, and a third from the Secretary-General.[1]

Here we put forward highlights and insights from a wide-ranging research effort by the United Nations Intellectual History Project (UNIHP). This summary presents findings from a long overdue effort to examine critically the UN's past in order to see its future more clearly. Understanding the past is essential to judge and take decisions on the host of recommendations for the United Nations in the 21st century. As George Santayana said, "Those who cannot remember the past are condemned to repeat it."

Fewer than one member in ten of today's human family was alive when the United Nations was founded in 1945. Even fewer were old enough to have followed those pioneering events in any detail. Sixty years later, the remarkable vision and creativity of the world organization's founders should be recalled.

The concern to see and understand the story as a whole led us to establish the United Nations Intellectual History Project in 1999. Six studies have been published, three more are in press, and five more are due out in the next two years. We have had access to a vast quantity of the UN's written records and the opportunity to interview many key participants in UN development efforts, including those who contributed so much to the UN's early years: all four living secretaries-general and some 50 others who have been a significant part of the UN's story. As former under-secretary-general Sir Brian Urquhart told us: "One of the troubles with the UN, which you are now rather belatedly remedying, is the fact that it never had a historical section. I spent years and years, from the time when I was the personal assistant to Trygve Lie, trying to get them to establish a historical section, so that people in all parts of the UN would actually record at the time what they were doing, instead of doing it 50 years later with a sort of esprit d'escalier."[2]

We added a question mark to the title of our first volume, *Ahead of the Curve?*, to indicate honest uncertainty about our early conclusions. Now with the benefit of further study, we feel less need to be tentative. The UN, in its economic and social development work, has many times been significantly in advance of governments, academics, and other international institutions that later adopted its ideas. The record clearly shows the pioneering nature of many of the UN's contributions. Three conclusions strike us:

- Although the UN receives more media attention for its efforts in peace and security, its contributions to ideas, analysis, and policymaking in the economic and social arena stand out as among its most important achievements.
- UN ideas and thinking in these arenas have had a major positive impact in many countries, those better off and those still very poor. There are also many areas where the UN ought to have made contributions but failed to do so—as well as others where the UN contribution was too little and too late.
- The successes and failures of the organization reflect the strengths and weaknesses of commitment and support from what we dub the "two United Nations"—the member states and the staff members. The contributions of many nongovernmental organizations (NGOs) to international conversations and norms have been significant enough on many occasions to refer to them as the "third UN."

The 14 commissioned UNIHP books add depth and detail to these broad conclusions. This report presents some of the highlights and concludes with suggestions to strengthen the UN's economic and social development work.

To grasp the full scale of the UN's achievements, one needs to see them in context. The need to avoid the slaughter and misery of more world wars and another Great Depression—as well as the failure of the first generation of universal organization, the League of Nations—were at the center of the vision that drove the hopes and focused the minds of those who created the world organization. The basic structures, designed during World War II and in the first decade or two afterwards, were all directed to these ends.

But what made the UN's design and establishment so remarkable was its broader ambition—for human rights on a global scale, for sovereign independence and freedom and democracy in all parts of the world, for improvements in living standards worldwide. Equally astonishing, when much of this lofty idealism was dismissed as little more than humbug, is that so much of this early vision has been achieved. No period in human history has seen so many people benefiting through advances in life expectancy, health, education, and living standards, as in the UN's lifetime.

Inevitably, the early hopes have wavered, especially when they have clashed with harsh realities of international politics and conflicting economic interests. Even so, the vision and early ambitions have never been entirely lost—and the UN has continued to refashion its goals and objectives through the ups and downs of subsequent decades.

The world organization's record over the last 60 years deserves to be better known. Policymakers dealing with it are often unaware both of what it has already achieved and what its shortcomings are in meeting intellectual challenges. Better awareness of the past would provide clearer perspectives of the UN's potential and ideas for what could and should be supported. Without this, many countries will continue to misjudge the UN's record and underestimate what it has done, and can do.

The UNIHP is now in mid-course, and others may interpret our findings differently. But as the orchestrators of this ambitious undertaking, we feel obliged to emphasize the most salient lessons for the UN's 60th anniversary. The key lessons:

- The intellectual contributions to ideas, analysis, and policy-making in the economic and social arenas have been among the UN's most important achievements. They have had a significant influence on national and international action. This can be judged by the extent to which UN ideas have often set paths that others have followed. Perhaps the clearest examples are global conferences setting goals and benchmarks that many countries have chosen to follow and that have influenced their policies and outcomes.
- The UN's original vision was built on four pillars. The first three—peace, development, and human rights—have become increasingly intertwined. Although initially separate, these three pillars now support a consistent and integrated frame of national and international priorities, applicable as guidelines for developed and developing countries. The annual *Human*

Development Report from the UN Development Programme (UNDP) elaborates a methodological frame for integrating, analytically and operationally, these three pillars of the UN.

- The UN's fourth founding pillar—sovereign independence for all countries—was largely achieved during the UN's first two decades. But it is now under scrutiny because of a concern for reasonable limits on state sovereignty in situations where human rights are under severe threat (as from genocide or civil war) or where human security is under threat (as from terrorism). This debate has already produced new ideas and norms, including the "responsibility to protect." Over time, additional principles should be incorporated into a broader and more consistent frame for development.

- The UN has a record of being boldly ahead of the curve, moving beyond conventional wisdom and sometimes confronting that wisdom with alternative thinking and policy proposals. This reflects at least in part its multidisciplinary and multisectoral structure and the egalitarian representation of countries in its governance structures. The UN has frequently been more ready than other international institutions to develop positions at variance with those of the major powers and to put its finger on issues not yet on the formal agenda. This comparative advantage should be encouraged. Pressures to be "politically correct" or "realistic"—from North or South, from diplomats or UN staff—should be resisted. Mistakes, of course, will be made. But what seems outlandish yesterday often becomes today's challenge and tomorrow's received wisdom.

- In the early 1980s there was an international shift of focus and financial support from the UN to the World Bank and the International Monetary Fund (IMF), leaving the UN with the role of constructive dissent rather than active initiative. The World Bank and sometimes the IMF have later adopted positions earlier pioneered or promoted by the UN—but which they initially opposed. There are many essential examples in the longer record—notably the Special UN Fund for Economic Development (SUNFED), leading to the World Bank's International Development Association (IDA) in the 1950s, and the goals for the development decade in the 1960s, for basic needs in the 1970s, and for poverty reduction today.

Three facts emerge from the UN's history in economic and social matters.

- The UN has contributed to economic and social thinking and widespread ideas of the second half of the 20th century.
- Many of these ideas have had a major and worthwhile impact.
- Many of the early ideas have emerged in response to initiatives of the dominant economic powers, especially those of the United States, even if Washington subsequently appears to have forgotten many of its early contributions. Gert Rosenthal

UN Constructive Dissent since the Early 1980s

Special support for the least developed countries was, as early as 1964, a focus of the UN Conference on Trade and Development (UNCTAD), which put forward proposals at the first of three international conferences in 1981. The neglect of these many proposals has in large part been responsible for the severe decline in many of these countries over the last two or three decades.

Economic adjustment policies in Sub-Saharan Africa and Latin America are now widely acknowledged to have been too narrow, too restrictive, or too rushed. The UN Children's Fund (UNICEF), the Economic Commission for Africa (ECA), and the International Labour Organization (ILO) argued for a broader approach from the mid-1980s.

Debt relief in the mid-1990s came too little and too late. UNCTAD and other organizations had analyzed the need for it in depth since 1985.

Transition policies in countries of Central and Eastern Europe and the former Soviet Union were front and center after the fall of the Berlin Wall in November 1989. The Economic Commission for Europe (ECE) proposed the need for a more gradual transition in 1989, to allow time for building up the new institutions required for a market-based system.

Good governance and democracy have been emphasized by the UN Development Programme since the 1980s but backed by inadequate funds.

Priorities for poverty reduction and basic needs were supported by the UN and the World Bank in the 1970s, but they fell off of the Bretton Woods' priorities until the mid-1990s. Meanwhile the UN had set and supported quantified, time-dated goals in a number of areas, which the Bank and the IMF adopted in the late 1990s.

The neglect of human rights by the Bretton Woods institutions and the UN's efforts to mainstream them are another example of the more comprehensive nature of development thinking in the world organization.

told us that the UN and its ideas influenced policy over time: "And all of a sudden, maybe two, three, five years after the document came out, everyone is repeating some of its main points as if they were gospel."

This introduction is followed by six short chapters. The first shows how the UN framed the issues. The second concentrates on how the UN led the way with new ideas and gradually broader and more realistic approaches to development. The third examines ideas that helped create a better atmosphere for international justice. The fourth looks at the importance of perspectives emanating from the world's major regions and civil society. The fifth suggests omissions and shows how the game of distorting ideas is played. The sixth puts forward our views about the intellectual challenges ahead.

CHAPTER 1

Framing the Issues

Beginning with its Charter, the United Nations has pursued a vision. And over the years, it has set out ideas and policy proposals that constitute an agenda to achieve that vision. As we pointed out in 2001, in the UNIHP's first volume, *Ahead of the Curve?,* the Charter incorporates four pillars, breathtaking in their boldness and universality:

- Peace—the idea that sovereign states could create an international organization and procedures that would replace military aggression and war by negotiation and collective security.

- Development—the idea that all countries, long independent or newly so, could purposefully pursue policies of economic and social advance, which over time would improve the welfare and living standards of their people.

- Human rights—the idea that every individual in every country throughout the world shared an equal claim not only to such individual civil and political rights as life, liberty, and the pursuit of happiness but also to a core of economic and social freedoms.

- Independence—the idea that people in all countries had rights to be politically independent and sovereign and make whatever national and international agreements that their citizens might choose.

Initially, these four pillars were pursued more in parallel than in an integrated fashion. Development was taken to be *economic* development. Mapping out what was involved was largely left to economists—often distinguished, it is true—but economists nonetheless, as opposed to other social scientists, historians, dyed-in-the-wool practitioners, or poets. Over subsequent decades, the UN's vision of development shifted, moving from the narrowly economic to a much broader and multidisciplinary perspective by the 1990s. Human development now incorporates human rights and conflict resolution. Peace-building is seen as an important ingredient in the construction of sustainable development, and development is seen as essential to promoting human security and human rights.

Today, the UN gives great emphasis to poverty reduction and, since the 147 heads of state and government met in 2000, to the Millennium Development Goals (MDGs). These goals are set in the broader frame of the Millennium Declaration,[3] a visionary document that makes clear that the goals for poverty reduction are only part of a much fuller agenda for sustainable development.

The UN's initial focus on an economic process was in line with thinking of the time. The UN issued three major reports on economic development in 1949 and 1951,[4] which provided us a powerful story in *Ahead of the Curve?* (pp. 26–42). The starting point for each report was how to achieve or maintain full employment, a preoccupation fired by the memories of the Great Depression in the 1930s and by Keynesianism. Soon though, this initial frame of reference gave way to a perspective more in line with the economic priorities and realities of developing countries. The second report was especially clear; *Measures for Economic Development of the Under-developed Countries* identified the rapid creation of employment as a fundamental goal, but then focused on long-term economic development as the condition for achieving it. The priority for poor countries was seen as raising savings, investment, and thus the rate of economic growth. The issue of diminishing income gaps between rich and poor countries was explicitly taken into account. Although the analysis was subtle and rich, the goal was narrow and in the end incomplete.

By the 1960s the importance of economic development was rising on the UN agenda, greatly stimulated by the many newly independent countries that had or were about to become member states. In 1961 U.S. President John F. Kennedy proposed, in a powerful speech to the General Assembly, that there should be a "development decade." His words even today ring fresh with insight:

> Political sovereignty is but a mockery without the means of
> meeting poverty and illiteracy and disease. Self-determination
> is but a slogan if the future holds no hope. This is why my
> Nation, which has freely shared its capital and technology to
> help others help themselves, now proposes officially designating the decade of the 1960s as the United Nations Decade of
> Development.[5]

Almost all parts of the world organization became involved in elaborating what the First Development Decade should include. Inputs came from some of the world's most prominent economists and other experts, including Arthur Lewis, Jan Tinbergen, Paul Hoffman, Barbara Ward, and Walt Rostow. *The UN Development Decade: Proposals for Action* was published in 1962. The "Foreword" by U Thant, then acting Secretary-General, makes clear that even then a more subtle perspective was beginning to emerge. "Development is not just economic growth, it is growth plus change."

The same report quoted the Economic and Social Council (ECOSOC):

> One of the greatest dangers in development policy lies in the tendency to give the more material aspects of growth an overriding and disproportionate emphasis. The end may be forgotten in preoccupation with the means. Human rights may be submerged and human beings seen only as instruments of production rather than as free entities for whose welfare and cultural advance the increased production is intended. The recognition of this issue has a profound bearing upon the formulation of the objectives of economic development and the methods employed in attaining them.[6]

In the 1970s the ILO led the way in shifting the focus to employment, but it was embedded in a much broader exploration of the development conundrum. Underlying an apparent "lack of jobs," the ILO pointed to three distinct types of employment problems: open unemployment in the Western sense; the frustration of job-seekers unable to obtain the type of work or the remuneration which they judged reasonable; and most important, a low level of incomes—in fact, poverty—obtained by many producers and their families, reflecting the under-utilization and low productivity of the labor force, both male and female.[7] This definition of the employment problem created the link between employment, poverty, income distribution, and development.

Over the 1970s, the path led to greater analysis and concern for poverty and to the ideas of redistribution with growth and basic needs. These formed the cutting edge for national development strategies, formally endorsed in the resolutions of the World Employment Conference in 1976. These ideas also had an important impact on the World Bank, where its president, Robert McNamara, and his chief economist, Hollis Chenery, strongly emphasized poverty reduction and, later in the 1970s, basic needs.

Within the UN the development agenda was being broadened further by a series of pioneering world conferences. These focused on environment and development (1972), hunger and world food problems (1974), population growth (1974), employment and basic needs (1976), human settlements (1976), and science and technology (1979). The first of the world conferences on women, in Mexico City in 1975, had an institutional and legal impact, creating two important UN institutions for women—UNIFEM (UN Development Fund for Women) and INSTRAW (International Research and Training Institute for the Advancement of Women). It also set in motion actions that led four years later to the Convention on the Elimination of All Forms of Discrimination against Women (CEDAW).

As Leticia Shahani, the deputy secretary-general of the Mexico Conference, told us during her interview about the conference's pioneering achievement: "For the first time, governments accepted the issue of women, the status of women, as a governmental concern. It wasn't just a social welfare [issue] handled only by NGOs. Now governments took a serious look at how half of the population in their societies live."

Nobel Prizes and the United Nations

Most observers think primarily about the peace and security dimension of the UN when the Nobel Prize is mentioned. And indeed, the Nobel Peace Prize has been awarded to Ralph Bunche, Dag Hammarskjöld, Kofi Annan, the Office of the UN High Commissioner for Refugees, UN peacekeepers, and the UN itself.

But the UN's economic and social institutions have made an impact. Two development agencies, the ILO and UNICEF, have also been recognized with Nobel Peace Prizes.

More important from the viewpoint of our intellectual history are the Nobel laureates in economics who have spent a substantial part of their professional lives working as UN staff members or contributing to UN ideas and activities. These are, in chronological order of receiving the Prize, Jan Tinbergen, Gunnar Myrdal, Wassily Leontief, James E. Meade, W. Arthur Lewis, Richard Stone, Lawrence Klein, Theodore W. Schultz, and Amartya Sen.

Moreover, among other Nobel laureates were Alva Myrdal who worked at the UN Educational, Scientific and Cultural Organization (UNESCO) for several years, John Boyd Orr, the first director-general of the Food and Agriculture Organization, René Cassin, who played a role in the UN's earliest work on human rights, and Ragnar Frisch, who shared the first Nobel Prize in economics with Jan Tinbergen in 1969 and collaborated with the UN on several occasions.

Ten years later, Nairobi was "a major breakthrough in what we can call the integration of women in development, and making the women's issue now a part of the entire development and peace process. And, of course, human rights . . . Nairobi was the first successful attempt in a UN global conference to put women's issues within the major concerns of the UN, as part of the economic and political picture."

In contrast to the consensus of these global conferences and the substantive ideas coming out of them, the sixth and seventh special sessions of the General Assembly in 1974 and 1975 led to fireworks. These responded to Third World calls for a New International Economic Order (NIEO). A stalemate on this theme continued until the end of the 1970s, when strong opposition from the industrial countries effectively removed it from the international agenda.

In the early 1980s, with rising debt and world recession, action on many of these broader perspectives came to a shuddering halt. Thus began what Enrique Iglesias, the president of the Inter-American Development Bank, called the "lost decade" for Latin America and Africa. The economic role of the UN diminished. From this point forward, the IMF and the World Bank, with strong support from the West, set the core international agenda for economic development, with a dominant focus, initially on stabilization, later on structural adjustment. These gave overwhelming priority to reducing inflation, correcting imbalances in deficits, and restoring economic growth, in that order of priority and often with space only for the first two. The development agenda narrowed once again.

In the 1980s the United Nations was left to take on the role of constructive dissent. In 1985 UNICEF began promoting the need for "adjustment with a human face."[8] In parallel ECA promoted calls for an African Alternative Framework for Structural Adjustment Programs.[9] By 1990 the world organization put forward a more active and comprehensive strategy, with the publication by the UN Development Programme of its first annual *Human Development Report,* setting out a fundamental alternative to Bretton Woods orthodoxy. Successive reports broadened the development agenda by exploring what a truly human development approach would mean for several priority areas: the concept and measurement of development, development financing, global income distribution, human security, women's equality and gender, economic growth, poverty, consumption, globalization, human rights, and cultural diversity. Each of these became less an add-on to economic development than an enrichment of the concept of human development.

The flavor of the times and the human development approach were captured by then ECA executive secretary Adebayo Adedeji who told us: "I had to unlearn a lot of what I was taught at Harvard, London, Leicester, and Ibadan. I came to realize that development is more than mere economism, more than macroeconomic aggregates and indicators, that human beings are not mere economic beings. They are also political, social, and cultural beings as well, and these affect their behavioral patterns in the economic domain. Therefore, what is needed to launch the development process on a sustainable basis is a holistic human development paradigm, not a narrow economic growth strategy. While economic growth is no doubt important, it is insufficient to bring about a holistic sustainable human development."

In the 1990s after the end of the Cold War came the second round of global conferences and summits, reinforcing earlier priorities for environment, human rights, population, social development, gender equality, food security, and urban development. These culminated in 2000 in the Millennium Summit, which adopted a program focused on poverty reduction and the achievement of the Millennium Development Goals by 2015. By this stage, new efforts had been made to establish closer links between the UN and the Bretton Woods institutions, which accepted the MDGs.

Over more than half a century, the four original pillars of the Charter (peace, development, human rights, and independence), largely pursued in parallel in the first few decades, came closer together, a remarkable and underemphasized advance. The integration of these important facets of the human challenge may be the most underrecognized achievement of the world organization. Fernando Henrique Cardoso, Brazil's former president and a distinguished social scientist, told us that the broadening of the concept of development to include social aspects was "a consequence of United Nations presence across the world in order to enlarge views on what the government role is, and also the concept of equitable development . . . All this, I think, has a direct effect on social science in general, even when the persons are not aware of the fact. But the renewal of the issues and themes was very important, a subject matter to be taken up by universities, and by political parties. I think this was a very important role played by the United Nations."

Human rights have now been integrated into a coherent philosophy of human development, providing a broader strategy for economic development and human progress. Conflict resolution has been accepted as an essential condition for development, with the Secretary-General issuing in 1992 *An Agenda for Peace*,[10] setting out international strategy for conflict prevention, peace-making, peace-building, and peace-keeping. This has been taken further recently with proposals emanating in 2004 from the High-level Panel on Threats, Challenges and Change to create a Commission on Peace-building, as a subcommittee of the Security Council.

Sovereign independence is the area where, over the decades, success in the original aim has been followed by some fundamental rethinking. With most colonies having become independent in the 1950s and 1960s, and a few more in the 1970s, the political drive to further independence somewhat faded while awareness of its limits increased. With the end of the Cold War, civil war in a number of former colonies also grew. Spurred by several hard-hitting speeches from the Secretary-General, genocide and other violent abuses of human rights led the UN to embark on a series of debates exploring "humanitarian intervention" and "the responsibility to protect."[11]

An Agenda for Development, issued in 1995, received little attention at the time but demonstrates the new integration within a formal definition of development:

> The goal of development is the improvement of human well-being and the quality of life. This involves the eradication of poverty, the fulfilment of basic needs of all people, and the protection of all human rights and fundamental freedoms, including the right to development. It requires that governments apply active social and environmental policies and that they promote and protect all human rights and fundamental freedoms on the basis of democratic and widely participatory institutions.[12]

Despite these positive moves to a fuller and more rounded perspective on development, several key issues, identified as major priorities in the early years of the United Nations, appear to have dropped out or faded away. These include moderating the causes of extreme instability in developing countries, especially those linked to fluctuations in commodity prices and other factors in international trade and finance; disarmament and development; and narrowing extreme gaps between the richest and poorest countries.

Strong and decisive action on any one of these three, let alone on two or three of them, might have changed the entire *problématique* of the poorest countries and of the global economy. For these reasons, ways need to be found to put these three issues, and no doubt others, back on the agenda. But before turning to the future, we provide some of the highlights of the UN's past contributions.

CHAPTER 2

Leading the Way

Many of the UN's pioneering contributions are so readily accepted today that it is often difficult to recall the extent of the controversy and the passion that accompanied their launch and adoption. Most important, the United Nations has been instrumental in widening the concept of development, making it more complicated—and more realistic. Development now includes human rights, human security, gender, environmental issues, population, sustainability, and culture. Measuring concretely the dimensions of the world has been another UN contribution. This chapter explores ideas and issues that made a difference and altered the way we conceive and quantify aspects of economic and social development.

Quantifying the World

National and international statistics are an arena of action that many nonspecialists take for granted. Moreover, many are quite unaware of the leading role of the UN over the years. In fact, the world organization's contribution to statistics has often been crucial in ensuring that necessary information is available for analyzing problems and making policies, nationally and internationally. The UN's work in this area often sets the frame for assessing the world's economic and social progress—or the lack of it.

Michael Ward, in *Quantifying the World: UN Ideas and Statistics*, has told the virtually unknown story of how ideas about what is to be measured have influenced statistical offices the world over and, in turn, had a major impact on economic perceptions, priorities, and actions. He concludes that: "The creation of a universally acknowledged statistical system and of a general framework guiding the collection and compilation of data according to recognized professional standards, both internationally and nationally, has been one of the great and mostly unsung successes of the UN Organization" (p. 2).

The Statistical Commission was established in 1945, in the UN's first few months. Its work soon achieved worldwide significance and had a global impact. A mass of common information became available to guide national and international action and policymaking. It is these data sets that make possible the assessment of comparative progress and performance, between countries or regions.

What a contrast with the situation before the creation of the United Nations! A glance at statistical reports from the 1930s reminds one of maps of the 16th and 17th century, with vast blank areas marked *terra incognita*. Today, a range of comparable data is available for almost all countries. Gross national product (GNP) is perhaps the measure most used for the size of a country's economy. Other measures chart critical areas of human progress including economic and social activities, environmental sustainability, and poverty reduction. In almost every case, the world body has had a hand in setting the standards underlying these statistical indicators and often in providing technical support to help establish the underlying national measurement systems and ensure their functioning well enough to do the job.

Equally important, the United Nations has played a major part in establishing a professional ethic of statistical independence and objectivity. It has encouraged public access to such information, nationally and internationally—especially with its regular statistical publications and its high-profile reports. This is an underemphasized contribution to building democracy.

Ward's account brings out the UN's central role in enabling the global statistical community to achieve "a degree of integration that should be the envy of others searching for common ground on which to build consensus. This was the work of people with vision. The development of an international statistical system is the outcome also of an honest open interchange between the main producers and users of data" (p. 3).

This said, the range of international statistics available today is still too often far from adequate—and part of the inadequacy reflects the world organization's limitations and failures along the way. In its early years the UN Statistical Office (UNSO) played an original and formative role, though as "less an original source of new statistical thinking than [as] . . . an efficient innovator" (p. 3). Activities in this field were guided by the Statistical Commission, which included some of the world's most eminent statisticians. It mobilized support from such distinguished professionals as the Indian statistician, P.C. Mahalanobis, and the Cambridge economist and later Nobel laureate, Richard Stone. Eleanor Roosevelt, it appears, ensured that "the establishment of a special information and statistical service on the 'status of women'" was the first item on its substantive agenda (p. 41).

The UN's early statistical work was greatly influenced by Keynesian thinking. This intellectual framework encouraged the belief that the major economic priority was to establish a system of national accounts in every country as the basis for pursuing policies of full employment and economic growth. The UN played the major role in developing, extending, and implementing in most countries the basics of national accounts and building up national statistical systems to provide for their preparation and regular publication.

While recognizing this enormous achievement, *Quantifying the World* explores a fascinating counterfactual—what might have been if alternative priorities had been adopted. While the issues of full employment and the restoration of stable growth assumed great prominence in postwar Europe, hunger and poverty were the overriding issues for developing countries. Different perceptions and priorities might have emerged if the alleviation of hunger and the reduction in the large number of poor people around the world had been given more direct emphasis, as they are being given—60 years later—in the Millennium Development Goals. In the event, Ward argues that serious international work on social statistics and indicators—fertility, gender, health, nutrition, hunger—was begun only in the 1970s and 1980s, and many statistical indicators to underpin strategies for poverty reduction only emerged in the mid-1990s (pp. 53 and 151).

Over the last two decades the UN Statistical Office has taken initiatives in the development of social statistics, statistics on women, and satellite accounts, a mechanism for linking environmental concerns to the main body of a country's national accounts. Such initiatives have, however, been limited, and many of the new statistical approaches have emerged from the work of some 10 "city groups," consultative groups of national technical experts working on such specific problems as household income statistics, capital stocks, informal sector statistics, environmental statistics, and poverty.

The UNSO lost some of its intellectual authority at a time when political interest and debate became intense on such critical issues as human rights, human security, the operation of transnational corporations, and many related areas of global performance and global governance. Ward concludes that the United Nations gave up "the crown jewels of statistical measurement and conceded control of statistical authority to institutions committed to supporting the economic and financial agenda of Western orthodoxy." Fortunately, he adds, "with the turn of the new millennium, the UN Statistical Office has moved back to center stage to begin forging new strategies," especially those relating to the problems of poverty reduction and human development. But there are still many areas of the broader agenda needing major international attention, most notably indicators of human rights performance; the measurement of overall resource depreciation; climate change and global warming; the global nature of deprivation, inequality, and wealth; the determinants of good governance; participation of civil society in decision making; and human security (pp. 4 and 40).

Setting Global Goals

Achievements must be judged by results—and for most purposes, goals for outputs are even more important than goals for inputs. One essential contribution of the world organization has been formulating, adopting, and promoting global development goals. Beginning with goals for education set around 1960 in three major regional conferences organized by UNESCO, the United Nations has formulated some 50 goals across the whole field of development. This contrasts sharply with the World Bank and the IMF, which not only have shied away from formulating global goals but, until the last few years, have not formally recognized them, even after their adoption by the international community of states. Moreover, in the case of the controversial structural adjustment programs in the 1980s, the Bretton Woods institutions resisted outcome goals country-by-country. Instead, they prioritized general economic indicators, such as the reduction in inflation and budgetary imbalances and the extent of liberalization and privatization.

In 1961 the UN took up John F. Kennedy's challenge for a development decade and formulated the first two global economic goals—an output goal that economic growth in developing countries should increase to 5 percent a year by 1970, and an input goal that total transfers (aid and private capital flows combined) from developed to developing countries should increase to 1 percent of the GNP of industrial countries. The goal for economic growth was exceeded—growth averaged 5.5 percent over the 1960s—even though it was thought by many to be excessively optimistic. The goal for transfers, though not fully achieved, had a considerable impact: total transfers reached almost 0.8 percent of industrial country GNP by 1970, four-fifths of the goal.

These numbers and the importance of target-setting are dissected by Richard Jolly, Louis Emmerij, Dharam Ghai, and Frédéric Lapeyre in *UN Contributions to Development Thinking and Practice* (pp. 247–75). Over the 1960s other goals were set—most notably, eradicating smallpox within 10 years, adopted by the World Health Assembly in 1966. This goal was achieved within 11 years. Over the 1970s, 1980s, and 1990s various UN bodies set other global goals with quantitative targets. The MDGs are the latest in a sequence that has extended over four decades. The elaboration of a strategy to accelerate progress by the Millennium Project under Jeffrey Sachs's direction marks a further step.

The value of setting goals is often questioned by those who see them as empty vessels. However, the record of achievement is more positive than this. *UN Contributions* reviewed all the goals that had a quantified target and a date fixed for their achievement. The 50 or so goals cover a wide range: faster economic growth, higher life expectancy, lower child and maternal mortality, better health, broader access to safe water and sanitation, greater access to education, less hunger and malnutrition, moves to sustainable development—and support for these efforts by the expansion of aid. Most of the goals were adopted after long and vigorous debate and careful scrutiny.

Of course, achieving goals or falling short is only indirectly a reflection of the UN's efforts—but the goals have provided a spur to national policies and a benchmark for success or failure. The record of achievement is better than many believe. Success with the economic growth goal in the First Development Decade led to a higher goal of 6 percent a year in the 1970s for the Second Development Decade. This goal was achieved by 35 countries, and the average growth was 5.6 percent, a bit higher than in the 1960s. After 1980 economic performance largely deteriorated, with the notable exception of China and several other East Asian countries and, in the 1990s, of India. Though the UN continued to set goals for economic growth, it averaged only 4 percent in developing countries in the 1980s and 4.7 percent in the 1990s, in both cases pulled up by the exceptional performance of the two giants, China and India.

The record for the key goals for human development has been considerably better. In 1980, the goal was set that life expectancy should reach 60 years at a minimum—a goal achieved in 124 of 173 countries. At the same time, the goal for reducing infant mortality by 2000 was set at 120 per 1,000 live births in the poorest countries and 50 in all others. By 2000, after impressive acceleration of immunization and other child survival measures, 138 developing countries had attained this goal. Progress in other areas has been considerable. Reductions in malnutrition, iron deficiency anaemia, and vitamin A deficiency advanced over the 1990s. Expansions of water and sanitation facilities over the 1980s more than doubled access in the decade.

Our review of progress for all 50 goals reveals that results have been generally positive but mixed, far from full achievement but rarely total failures. Progress on economic growth has slipped badly over the decades, with average growth among developing countries only marginally better in the 1990s than in the 1980s, but in both cases below the rates in the 1960s and 1970s.

UN Contributions makes clear that the most serious failures have been in Sub-Saharan Africa and the least developed countries. But even here, performance on the human goals has often been considerably better than on the targets for economic growth or international aid. The least developed countries, today numbering 49, were set the target of doubling their national income over each of the last century's two closing decades. In support, developed countries were set the goal of providing aid amounting to 0.15 to 0.20 percent of their GNP. The failure in economic performance was the most serious of all the goals. Only three least developed countries, with only 1 percent of their total population, achieved the growth target. Only eight donor countries achieved the aid target in the 1980s, only five in the 1990s. Total aid to the least developed countries had fallen to 0.05 percent of individual country GNP in the 1990s, down from 0.09 percent in the 1980s (pp. 259–67). Fortunately, in the new millennium there are signs of some recovery in the allocation of aid to these countries.

Human Rights

"Promoting respect for, and observance of, human rights and fundamental freedoms for all"—as set out in Charter Article 62—was a revolutionary idea in 1945. Of the four pillars underlying the UN, it was the boldest idea of all.

Over the UN's first two decades, the ideas of individual rights and fundamental freedoms gave rise to many conflicts, clashing time and again with the reality of state interests. Such battles continue, though the positions of protagonist countries and opposition countries have frequently shifted—and continue to shift today.

In the early days of the UN, the initial architects of human rights were the major powers of the postwar world—the United States, the United Kingdom, and the Soviet Union. All three were quietly conscious of major contradictions in their positions. The United States had deep domestic violations in various racist laws and practices. The Soviets had the gulags. And the British had their colonies.

Notwithstanding these contradictions, progress was remarkable—although the process of advance was confusing, repetitive, and sometimes marginal to the United Nations as a whole. In 1948 the Universal Declaration of Human Rights was born. In the mid-1960s the International Covenants on Political and Civil Rights and on Economic, Social, and Cultural Rights brought legal force to the elements in the Universal Declaration. In 1979 came CEDAW, and a decade later the Convention on the Rights of the Child.

Advances in human rights over the last half century reflect a story of individuals, NGOs, and states. But individuals and NGOs almost always have led the way or provided the pressure, with states initially opposed or reluctantly going along but eventually agreeing and providing legitimacy. This story is told in *The UN and Human Rights Ideas: The Unfinished Revolution,* by Sarah Zaidi and Roger Normand. The 1948 adoption of the Universal Declaration of Human Rights by the (then) 59 member states was hailed as an unprecedented achievement in international relations. Eleanor Roosevelt, who chaired the Commission on Human Rights that oversaw its birth, often called the Declaration "the conscience of humanity." It undoubtedly remains the most cited piece of human rights documentation of the last century.

Its birth was anything but smooth or uncontested. There were profound ideological differences as to what constituted human rights and fundamental freedoms. The U.S. position was articulated by Eleanor Roosevelt, who wanted a non-legally binding declaration—"a statement of basic principles of inalienable human rights, setting up a common standard of achievement for all peoples and all nations."[13] The United Kingdom wanted a legally binding document, but one restricted to political and civil rights, with no mention of economic, social, or cultural rights. The Soviet Union argued that a declaration asserting general norms without legal specifics would be useless and abstract. But it was equally opposed to any internationally enforceable treaty, arguing that implementation was a matter of national sovereignty, guaranteed under the domestic jurisdiction of the Charter. Only Australia and India made the case for an enforceable and effective treaty with any conviction.

The Universal Declaration of Human Rights was agreed after two years. But it took a further 18 years of debate, sustained lobbying, and intense negotiation to reach the next step—the two international covenants that together with the Declaration constitute an "International Bill of Rights." These conventions were open for state parties to sign and ratify—and by 2004 some 151 countries had ratified the first and 148 the second covenant. The treaty-based system of implementation was itself an innovative idea in the field of human rights, arguably without precedent. It introduced two important issues: the obligation of the state to execute the legally binding articles, and the role of the international community in enforcing execution for a laggard state. Execution was seen as bringing domestic legislation into line with articles and ratifying the covenant.

Both the Universal Declaration of Human Rights and the covenants owe much to committed individuals, such as John Humphrey, the first director of the UN Division of Human Rights, Henri Laugier, the UN's assistant secretary-general in charge of social affairs, and members of the UN Commission on Human Rights, including René Cassin, who in 1942 had urged the creation of an international court to punish war crimes. Humphrey in his memoirs commented that "a determined group of individuals can influence an international conference and in matters of human rights, individuals and governments are usually on the opposite side of the ring."[14]

Over 60 years the United Nations has overseen the negotiation and birth of many other conventions covering, most notably, genocide (1948), racial discrimination (1965), and torture and other cruel, inhuman, or degrading treatment of punishment (1984). The UN Declaration on the Right to Development (1986) established an "inalienable human right by virtue of which each person and all peoples are entitled to participate in, contribute to, and enjoy economic, social, cultural, and political development in which all human rights and fundamental freedoms can be fully realized."

The World Conference on Human Rights, held in Vienna in 1993, forged what Secretary-General Boutros Boutros-Ghali called "a new vision of global action for human rights into the next century." The Vienna conference also succeeded in establishing UN machinery for overseeing implementation with the creation of the Office and also the post of High Commissioner for Human Rights, an international champion who can influence government action through fact-finding, quiet diplomacy, persuasion, and publicity.

Despite the doubts and opposition, the setbacks and inconsistencies, the progress in human rights since 1945 has been remarkable and unprecedented. This achievement is often missed because of the remaining massive violations of human rights that tend to hit the headlines. Yet the record is one of extraordinary advance. In 1900 no country had universal adult suffrage; today nearly all countries do. Between 1974 and 1999 multiparty electoral systems were introduced in 113 countries; only in some 40 countries are they lacking today. In 1990 only 10 percent of countries had ratified all seven

Human Rights Landmarks

1948 Universal Declaration of Human Rights

1948 ILO Convention on the Freedom of Association and Protection of the Right to Organize

1950 European Convention on Human Rights

1960 Inter-American Commission on Human Rights holds its first session

1961 Amnesty International established

1965 UN Convention on the Elimination of All Forms of Racial Discrimination

1966 UN International Covenant on Civil and Political Rights

1966 UN International Covenant on Economic, Social, and Cultural Rights

1967 Pontifical Commission for International Justice and Peace established

1968 First World Conference on Human Rights, in Tehran

1973 UN International Convention on Suppression and Punishment of the Crime of Apartheid

1979 UN Convention on the Elimination of All Forms of Discrimination against Women

1981 African Charter on Human and People's Rights

1983 Arab Commission for Human Rights

1984 UN Convention against Torture and Other Cruel, Inhuman and Degrading Treatment or Punishment

1986 UN Declaration on the Right to Development

1989 UN Convention on the Rights of the Child

1993 Second World Conference on Human Rights, in Vienna

1993 First UN High Commissioner for Human Rights appointed

1998 Rome Statute for establishing the International Criminal Court

1999 CEDAW Optional Protocol for Individual Complaints

2000 Millennium Declaration and adoption of Millennium Development Goals

major human rights instruments; today it is well over half. About 90 percent of all countries have ratified CEDAW and all but two countries the Convention on the Rights of the Child. Access to education, health services, basic nutrition, water, and sanitation are central to both these conventions, and here again the record shows more practical achievements over the last half century than ever before in history.[15] The Millennium Development Goals are commitments to carry forward these rights through practical actions.

The record also reveals important paths not taken. The Subcommission on Freedom of Information met only five times and died without a whimper in 1952. A commission on cultural rights was proposed but dropped. The agenda for the future still contains a long list. The High-level Panel has proposed that membership of the Commission on Human Rights be universal and that governments designate prominent and experienced human rights figures as the heads of their delegations. Both are intended to energize the next phase of international human rights advance, but universal membership would hardly improve effectiveness, which undoubtedly explains why the Secretary-General proposed instead the creation of a smaller and more credible Human Rights Council.

In summary, and as Zaidi and Normand make clear, the UN's leadership in human rights has achieved considerable success. Without doubt, it has changed the public policy discourse in all parts of the world. Ideas of human rights have provided a tactical guide to policy and action. They have helped form new coalitions of political and institutional forces. And they have become embedded in institutions, helping to define principles for action and future agendas. More broadly, one can see that worldwide public opinion toward human rights enforcement has been strengthened and the veil of sovereign immunity slowly stripped from governments.

Sustainability

Sustainable development became a leading theme in 1987 when the World Commission on Environment and Development published *Our Common Future*.[16] Three parts of the equation for the sustainability of the planet—resource management, environment, and population—have been topics in which UN ideas have contributed in essential ways to our ways of conceiving global responses.

A key document in the debate about global resource management is the 1962 UN Declaration on Permanent Sovereignty over Natural Resources, also referred to as the economic pendant of the decolonization declaration.[17] This and subsequent resolutions detail the rights of countries, including the right to manage freely natural resources for the benefit of the population and national economic development. The next step was to extend the resource sovereignty over marine resources as well. This resulted in a thorough revision of the traditional law of the sea.

The Third UN Conference on the Law of the Sea (1973–82) gave rise to an international deep-sea-bed regime based on the nascent principle of common heritage of humankind, as opposed to "first come, first served."[18] Nico Schrijver's forthcoming *The UN and the Global Commons: Development without Destruction* demonstrates that the new international resource regime of the law of the sea has proven irreversible and is providing coastal developing countries with considerable protection against distant fishing fleets and mining companies.

The capacity of the world to achieve and sustain development depends very much on dealing with *environmental* problems, little mentioned until the 1970s. As early as 1969 the Secretary-General had alerted the General Assembly to the problems of the human environment: "For the first time in the history of mankind, there is arising a crisis of worldwide proportion involving developed and developing countries—the crisis of the human environment."[19] In 1972 the UN organized in Stockholm the Conference on the Human Environment—it was path-breaking, politically and conceptually. Despite growing awareness of increasing pollution in the industrial countries and fears that scarcities of raw materials would, in the words of the first report to the Club of Rome, set "limits to growth,"[20] plans for the conference were initially met with massive criticism from several industrial countries and strong skepticism from developing countries.

To lead and organize its work, Maurice Strong, the Canadian industrialist who championed environment and development issues in a number of UN assignments, was appointed secretary-general of the conference. He gathered a group of experts from both North and South at Founex (near Geneva) to explore the issues. As Ignacy Sachs, who was there, told us, "The Stockholm conference emphasized the idea that development and environment management are complementary. To those who claimed that to protect the environment it was necessary to stop growth, the conference replied that there was an alternative, namely to change the pattern of growth and the use of its benefits. The outcome of Stockholm was a comprehensive program integrating economic, social, and political dimensions." He also noted, somewhat more cynically, that "It's not with environmental ministers that you achieve sustainable development." The group in Founex focused on squaring the circle—the big differences between the environmental and development priorities of developed and developing countries.

Common ground in this conflict was found by shifting the emphasis to the need for a new strategy that combined priorities for environment *and* development. These were included in the conference declaration, which called for the elimination of mass poverty and the creation of a decent and human environment. Some environmental problems would inevitably arise as a consequence of industrialization, but they should and could be minimized through appropriate policies. This was a major advance in thinking and political agreement. To carry the ideas forward, the conference agreed that a new body, the UN Environment Programme, be established.

Through the establishment of the World Commission on Environment and Development, the UN made an effort to develop a more integrated approach to this issue. Building on an earlier notion of sustainable use of natural resources,[21] the world organization defined sustainable development as "development which meets the needs of the present without compromising the ability of future generations to meet their own needs." All this was carried through to the Earth Summit in Rio in 1992 and the World Summit on Sustainable Development in Johannesburg in 2002.

By this time, a better understanding of environmental problems had emerged. The emphasis had shifted from absolute scarcity of certain non-renewable resources to the pollution or destruction of *renewable* resources, especially water and air, soil, and forests. As ever more evidence of climate change emerged, global warming became one of the world's most recognized and serious environmental problems. Until then, environmental problems were seen as those of how to survive in a global fish bowl. In 1997 the UN conference in Kyoto introduced the problem of what to do when the goldfish bowl is put into a microwave. Kyoto came into force in early 2005.

In 1945 the world's people numbered just under 2.5 billion—today, well over 6 billion, by far the largest and fastest expansion in human history. Even so, population growth was not treated as a major policy issue for the UN's first two decades. Analytically, the world organization issued a comprehensive and pioneering volume in 1953, *The Determinants and Consequences of Population Trends,*[22] which contained data and analysis far ahead of the time. Indeed, in those years many countries lacked even a basic census, let alone population forecasts or policy analyses. The UN's volume also included wildly inaccurate projections that the world population would reach between 3.3 and 3.8 billion by the year 2000. But policy discussion on matters of population was played down as highly sensitive and essentially kept off the international agenda.

A slow awakening occurred in the 1960s. In 1966 the Economic and Social Commission for Asia and the Pacific (ESCAP) organized a meeting on the management of family planning. ECOSOC devoted two sessions in the late 1960s to the issues. The United Nations Fund for Population Activities was established in 1969. Then in 1974 the UN organized its first World Population Conference in Bucharest. After this, concrete action embedding ideas in new institutions and policy measures became commonplace. Within less than 10 years, about 70 percent of the participating countries had established high-level units to deal with population issues. By 1994 fertility rates were falling in most countries outside the poorest, and the UN organized a further conference—the International Conference on Population and Development in Cairo. This put the emphasis on a much broader agenda, shifting it from family planning to women's empowerment, gender equality, the right to choose, and improving maternal and reproductive health. Although the world's population is now projected to grow to about 8.5 billion by 2050, fertility rates in countries with almost half the world's population have now fallen to below replacement levels. As Nafis Sadik told us, "I had always had this idea of linking women's rights with family planning. But to broaden the whole subject from family planning to reproductive health, and make it into a rights approach has evolved." Clearly research and measurement have political ramifications.

Three points should be noted (and will be stressed by Schrijver). First, the UN has been instrumental in generating widespread interest in national resource management by taking account of economic, social, and environmental dimensions. Second, new concepts of resource management have been introduced, such as resource sovereignty, the global commons, sustainable use of natural resources, and sustainable development. Third, the UN has given a major push to put population and environment problems high on the national agendas through the world conferences of the 1970s and 1990s.

Many practical initiatives have followed from these conferences, and progress has been considerable, including the adoption of UN conventions on the Law of the Sea and the Prevention of Marine Pollution by Dumping, and the protection of the ozone layer (1985).

The 1992 Rio conference led to further conventions on climate change, biodiversity, and desertification, along with the creation of the Global Environment Facility, to provide funding and technical assistance for projects to preserve biodiversity, protect forests, and improve soils. In 1997, with ever more evidence of global warming, the Kyoto Protocol was adopted to strengthen the provisions of the convention on climate change. Despite the progress, almost all evidence suggests that global warming is advancing fast, with governments still unwilling to provide the support and funding to deal with the damage and degradation to many of the world's critical renewable resources, in both developed and developing countries.

Gender Equality

Four women were among the 160 or so delegates in San Francisco in 1945. Though miniscule in numbers, this group parlayed its influence into ensuring that equality between the sexes was part of the founding ideas of the new world organization. The Charter uses the phrase "men and women" 10 times. The "founding mothers," as pioneer Hilkka Pietilä refers to them, "laid the ground work for the struggle for gender equality that has since gained momentum throughout the world."[23] As Devaki Jain points out in *Women, Development, and the UN: A Sixty Year Quest for Equality and Justice,* the Charter is considerably more straightforward about gender equality in its language than the international conventions that preceded it, even though only about half the UN member states then gave women unrestricted rights to vote and hold public office.

Almost immediately, the UN established the Commission on the Status of Women (CSW) as a separate body for advancing women's rights within the organization. Created as a sub-commission of ECOSOC, it was led by a Danish woman, Bodil Begtrup, who argued that having such a commission would enable women's problems for the first time to be studied at an international level. Many member states were hesitant to internationalize the issue of women's inequality, arguing that this was to intrude into sovereignty. In sharp contrast, a handful of daring women argued that women be given full political suffrage world-wide, entering what was till then distant, if not taboo, political territory. Their founding belief was that "political rights and development are fundamental." They succeeded. By 1952, the UN had adopted the Convention on Political Rights of Women and put the campaign for suffrage for women on a legal footing. This convention stated that women should be entitled to vote in all elections, be eligible for election to all publicly elected bodies, and be entitled to hold public office. The CSW had already been active in calling for the United Nations to collect the facts, which it did in a survey of 74 countries.

Even with this progress on political rights, the situation of women was ignored in most of the UN's work on economic and social development. The declaration on the UN's First Development Decade and its proposals for action made no mention of women—though in 1962 the General Assembly instructed the CSW "to prepare a report on the role of women in the social and economic development plans of member governments." Even within the CSW, there was an opinion that development was not really a women's issue and that too much attention to economic development would divert the commission from its primary goal of securing women's rights. It preferred "to emphasize the human element in development and called for greater investment in women as human resources."[24]

The big changes for women in economic and social development started in the 1960s. In 1963 the General Assembly asked the CSW and ECOSOC to draft a Declaration on the Elimination of Discrimination against Women—and DEDAW was adopted four years later, the first comprehensive legal measure on women's rights. Among the regional commissions, the Economic Commission for Africa was in the lead, supporting several path-breaking seminars and conferences on women in development and in 1967 issuing the *Status and Role of Women in East Africa*.[25]

Margaret Snyder, who was UNIFEM's first executive head, told us: "In 1960/1961, they had 'Role of Women in Community Development' and 'Role of Women in Urban Development.' In 1964–65 they spoke of the need for a study of population growth and the role of women in development. This was much before anybody was talking about women in development . . . Helvi Sepila of Finland later said ECA had the lead in all of the regions toward the achievement of equal rights for men and women as set forth in the UN Charter . . . No other region did anything for women at that stage . . . What was making ECA a leader in this was that the concepts were very different from any at the UN or any others at the time, because we were talking about women as part of the active labor force."

The publication in 1970 of *Women's Role in Economic Development* by the Danish economist Esther Boserup—who worked in the Economic Commission for Europe—marked an intellectual breakthrough, launching the field of women in development. Her view that women's contributions, both domestic and in the paid workforce, constituted crucial contributions to national economies electrified women scholars and gave birth to a new development approach in the UN and other development agencies.

The four world conferences on women—1975 in Mexico City, 1980 in Copenhagen, 1985 in Nairobi, and 1995 in Beijing—raised awareness and mobilized action at a new level, especially by establishing or extending networks and alliances in novel ways. The Mexico conference in 1975 led to the adoption of CEDAW and in 1976 of UNIFEM and INSTRAW. However significant the contributions of these institutions, *Women, Development, and the UN* shows that the four UN women's conferences have strengthened the worldwide women's movement and given it a new level of impact, influence, and focus.

The changing focus on women also brought changes in thinking about development. The conceptualization of women's work shifted—to incorporate work outside the marketplace and care as key though often forgotten elements of family and community life. This raised questions and challenged how economic and social contributions should be valued. It brought the need to rethink rights to development, not just of women but rights more generally.

Jain's analysis emphasizes the changing dynamics of understanding. Progress means more than simple advance by past yardsticks. As the women's movement makes clear, each forward step requires re-thinking the next, as progress continues. Each mountain climbed transforms the landscape and reveals yet another peak, higher still on the horizon. Indeed, she told us during her interview: "In Beijing the biggest pledge was that women have to come into power because it is only through power that you renegotiate the discrimination which you face . . . When you analyze it from a feminist point of view, you actually challenge the very facts and theoretical propositions of that particular theory—economic theory, statistical classificatory systems, measuring tools, measurement hierarchies. So you are opening up a new world of how to analyze. We also argue that this form of analysis is useful not only for women, but for all forms of people discriminated against . . . It's a form of looking at a new picture of discrimination and how it is embedded."

Human Development

UNDP's annual *Human Development Report* came on the scene in 1990, elaborating the approach inspired by Mahbub ul Haq, an economic visionary and former minister of finance of Pakistan. There had been much general talk of "human development" in the 1980s and of "putting people at the center of development." But it was the creative economic thinking and philosophy of Amartya Sen, who received the 1998 Nobel Prize in economic sciences, that gave the human development approach its robust theoretical foundations. "Human development" was defined analytically as a process of strengthening human capabilities and expanding human choices. Though deceptively simple, the concept marked a fundamental contrast to the utilitarianism underlying neoclassical economics. Moreover, it provided a frame of reference that could be elaborated and applied to a wide range of development issues, as successive reports have demonstrated.

As Sen recounted in *UN Voices:* "The Human Development Reports, under Mahbub ul Haq's visionary leadership, consolidated the criticisms that had emerged in the literature on heavy reliance on the GNP and such commodity-based indicators, which was standard practice when Mahbub got going. I remember his first phone call to me on this in 1989. We had to focus instead, Mahbub argued, on the lives of human beings—their freedoms and well-being, their capabilities." In addition to Haq and Sen, the team included a host of other intellectual stalwarts (Paul Streeten, Meghnad Desai, Keith Griffin, Gus Ranis, Frances Stewart, and Sudhir Anand).

Sen also pointed to a downside: "One slightly negative side of this approach, which relied heavily on public relations, was that in order to win the attention of the public, Mahbub had to simplify tremendously. He went on to do things which were exactly right for his purpose, but also generated a good deal of problems for the intellectual respectability of the 'human development approach.' One of them was his insistence on having one very simple 'Human Development Index,' or the HDI."

"Anyway the HDI which we devised did become quite popular, despite its arbitrariness," Sen continued. "Mahbub was immensely skilled in getting the attention of the world. He was out to 'get the GNP,' and he did. Even though I had been very opposed to having one simple Human Development Index, I ended up gladly helping him to develop it, since he persuaded me that there was no way of replacing the GNP unless we had another similarly simple index. But this index will be better in the sense that it will focus on human lives, and not just on commodities."

The importance of the idea of human development is central to the stories told in almost all of the UNIHP's volumes. Why? Human development built on the priorities of basic needs thinking in the 1970s but went substantively beyond them by adopting Sen's framework of capabilities and freedom.[26] In addition, human development provided a frame of analysis that brought human rights and development closer together. As the 2000 report showed, human development adds value to human rights by setting rights in a frame of dynamic economic and social advance. In turn, human rights adds value to human development by bringing in legal precision and legitimacy. By developing four proxy indices for the measurement of human development—not only the HDI but also the gender development index (GDI), the gender empowerment measure (GEM), and the human poverty index (HPI)—the human development approach has achieved widespread attention, especially with its controversial annual publication of the rankings of almost all the world's countries.[27]

In addition to elaborating on the idea of basic needs, human development provided a framework for many UN institutions and governments to change policies and take practical steps. Examples abound. There is now, once again, central emphasis on poverty reduction in development policies, including those of the World Bank and IMF. We observe a growing diversification in development strategies with more emphasis on cultural factors. Social policies—education, health, nutrition—are getting more attention. The adoption of the Millennium Development Goals in 2000 and the revisiting of progress at the summit preceding the 60th session of the General Assembly in 2005 are perhaps the most prominent indications.

Human development has been a successful UN counter-offensive to the Washington Consensus, after the hesitations during the 1980s. It redefines the idea of development broadly yet realistically. Development is seen as a complex challenge, one that embraces far more than economic variables and faster growth. These are important factors, but far from the whole story. Development is a process that advances human rights, human capabilities, and human choices, with people at the center. More details are found throughout *UN Contributions to Development Thinking and Practice*.

Human Security

Possibilities for creatively linking development and disarmament have been recognized and recommended over every decade of the world organization's existence. In 1955 France made the first proposal at the United Nations. Participating states should agree to reduce their military spending each year by a fixed percentage, with the resources released paid into an international fund, a quarter allocated to development and the remainder left at the disposal of the government. Variants of this proposal emerged from other governments in subsequent decades, including the First Development Decade in the 1960s.[28]

The most thorough and innovative report on disarmament and development came later when the Thorsson Commission was set up in 1982. Its report, after reviewing the evidence and analyzing the issues, concluded that "the world can continue to pursue the arms race with characteristic vigor or move consciously and with deliberate speed toward more stable and balanced economic and social development. It cannot do both."[29]

This long and outspoken concern of the UN for disarmament and development contrasts with the years of silence from the World Bank and the IMF. As the World Bank historians commented, "Arms reduction . . . is sensitive as well as political and was typically avoided by the Bank until . . . the aftermath of the Cold War."[30] Interestingly, the Bank's former president and U.S. secretary of defense, Robert McNamara, became a fervent advocate for tying investments to disarmament. The 1980 Nobel laureate in economics, Lawrence Klein, has long been involved in analyzing the waste of arms expenditures and emphasized the world organization's efforts in his interview with us, including the quest for the elusive "peace dividend."

A major conceptual shift came in 1994, when UNDP's *Human Development Report* articulated the concept of human security: "[F]or too long, the concept of security has been shaped by the potential for conflict between nations . . . equated with the threats to a country's borders . . . [with nations seeking] arms to protect their security."[31] In contrast, the report argued for "human security" to become the focus, shifting priorities to the protection of people rather than borders, to the use of police, health, and other community workers rather than armies and weapons, and to prevention rather than cure. A human security approach should tackle a diversity of threats to people's lives—the threats from disease and famine, from drugs and urban crime, from terrorism and ethnic conflict. The report also covered freedom from job insecurity and environmental threats.

Human security remains controversial for reasons that S. Neil MacFarlane and Yuen Foong-Khong bring out clearly in *Human Security and the UN: A Critical History*. Some critics believe that human security is little more than renaming as security a range of problems that already have perfectly good names. Others argue that the concept is so broad and fuzzy that it is meaningless, or loses "analytical traction" according to MacFarlane and Foong-Khong. In contrast, proponents argue that the world has entered a period when the range of security threats has been growing rapidly. Human security provides a framework for systematically examining the diversity of these threats and weighing the various responsive actions against each other.

Notwithstanding the controversy, human security is an idea that appears to be gaining ground. For instance, the High-level Panel on Threats, Challenges and Change incorporated many of these ideas in its call for "comprehensive, collective security." The panel identified six clusters of threats—beginning with economic and social threats (including poverty, infectious diseases, and environmental degradation) and listing five others: interstate conflict, internal conflict (including civil war and genocide), weapons (nuclear, radiological, chemical, and biological), terrorism, and transnational organized crime. These are all cases, the panel argued, where threats today required collective international action, preventive and reactive. Human security, it concluded, should be a central focus of actions for strengthening the UN in the world of the 21st century.

The authors of *Human Security and the UN* fall between enthusiasts and critics. They conclude their forthcoming book with the following passage:

> There has been a profound change in how security is conceived by international organizations and states. This evolution has recognized the security needs of individuals and the responsibilities of states and organization in attending to those needs. There has been a substantial accretion of norms designed to put that changed understanding into practice. It is reasonable to suppose that this evolving normative framework is reasonably durable in the face of shocks such as the advent of the threat from terrorism.

CHAPTER 3

Struggling for Justice and Opportunity

From the beginning, the United Nations has emphasized that international action must accompany and complement national efforts if development is to be equitable and global poverty reduced. An enabling international environment is required for alternative trade and finance measures to work and for other areas of economic interactions to improve between poorer and richer countries. Some of the UN's ideas in this area, though often controversial and challenging to conventional thinking, have been among its most creative.

Trade, Finance, and Development

Fresh thinking on trade and finance distinguishes the UN's contributions from the views of the Bretton Woods institutions and the dominant policies of the developed countries over the last half-century. It has been and remains an area of almost continuous tension. Typically, the world organization produces analysis and proposals to accelerate economic and social progress in developing countries. Meanwhile, the developed countries argue for free trade but use their political and economic power to practice something charitably described as "fair trade with important exceptions," or more simply as "unfair trade."

Long-run trends and fluctuations in exports, imports, and international trade were among the first areas for UN scrutiny. What began as backroom statistical calculations soon became important points of international debate, along with their repercussions on international political relations, international income distribution, and the structure of the world organization itself. John Toye and Richard Toye dug deeply into various archives to trace this original story in *The UN and Global Political Economy: Trade, Finance, and Development*.

One of the crucial parts of their tale includes the origins of what has become known as the Prebisch-Singer thesis: the tendency over the long run for the prices of coffee, tea, copper, cotton, and other primary product exports to decline relative to the prices of manufactures. Hans Singer, one of the pioneering economists of the UN who studied under both Schumpeter and Keynes, started his work in response to a priority identified at the first meeting of the UN Sub-Commission on Economic Development in 1947. He investigated the changes in prices of primary product exports relative to manufactured imports for underdeveloped countries. There was a short-term improvement during World War II, but for the half century before this, there had been a long-term secular decline, by about a third. Singer immediately grasped the significance. A secular decline of this magnitude would represent a large loss in the capacity of underdeveloped countries to generate the foreign exchange resources required for their development. It would also be a force for growing inequality in the world distribution of income.

The scene then moved to Latin America, where Raúl Prebisch shifted the emphasis from long-run changes in the terms of trade to the implications for policy. In order to escape from the impact of this secular decline in prices, what were then called "underdeveloped countries" would need to industrialize as the only means of fully obtaining the advantages of technical progress. Prebisch presented his conclusions—"a manifesto urging Latin American countries to launch into industrialization," in the words of the late Celso Furtado—to the Economic Commission for Latin America (ECLA) conference in Havana in 1950. According to the Toyes, they were greeted with acclaim by the Latin American delegates (pp. 123–24).

Debates about the thesis continued for decades. As with most long-run tendencies, every fluctuation around the trend could be hailed as a reason for doubting any long-run tendency. But with the terms of trade continuing their decline over the following half century, and in the light of the prices of many primary products reaching all-time lows around the end of the millennium (oil prices excluded), the Prebisch-Singer thesis is now generally accepted.

Industrialization as the universal remedy has had a more checkered career. Prebisch and ECLA argued for import-substituting industrialization as a decisive element in development strategy over the 1950s and early 1960s. This was not as simplistic as sometimes caricatured but was formulated within the broader context of geopolitics. Nor did they argue for protecting industry at any cost and without any limits. Excessive protectionism, for too long, was bound to lead to a skewed and unsustainable industrialization.

By the early 1960s Prebisch moved to a bigger stage with more limelight. Misgivings about the world trading system were welling up, and in 1962 Prebisch headed the preparations for the UN Conference on Trade and Development. He became its first secretary-general in 1964 after the completion of the largest international conference on trade ever convened. Cast as a drama of "global collective bargaining" between rich and poor, the "conference" became a permanent fixture in North-South relations, and UNCTAD itself became a permanent part of the UN's institutional structure.

The Toyes recount the story of how and why Prebisch envisaged UNCTAD not as a passive secretariat but as "an activist body," "an instrument for change," and "a fighting institution." He argued that it was possible and legitimate for UNCTAD to be both committed and impartial, looking for arrangements that would favor the position of developing countries. "Now, I have to be impartial towards all parties in the United Nations community," Prebisch said at one point, "and we are striving to be impartial at all times. But as for neutrality, we are not more neutral to development than WHO [the World Health Organization] is neutral to malaria."

Since these early days of hope, UNCTAD has continued, although somewhat weakened. This was especially so during the late 1980s after efforts, led by the West, to close it down. UNCTAD has filled an important and often pioneering gap in international analyses of trade and finance, producing significant reports and, at times, innovative proposals, albeit with much less success than hoped for. Unlike the General Agreement on Tariffs and Trade (GATT) and more recently the World Trade Organization (WTO), its focus has been on actions in trade and finance that aim to accelerate progress in the developing countries, with increasing emphasis in the last two decades on the special needs of the least developed countries.

In the 1970s UNCTAD focused on the needs for commodity agreements and proposed the creation of the Integrated Program for Commodities and the Common Fund to provide the support needed to bring them into existence. It also negotiated the Generalized System of Preferences, which in principle promised benefits to developing countries, but in the way it was put into effect became, in the eyes of many, a backward step. A third effort was to argue for an automatic link between the creation of Special Drawing Rights by the IMF and the allocation of some proportion of the money thus created to aid for developing countries. This proposal would have generated additional resources for the poorer countries without requiring additional aid from the developed world (pp. 236–38).

Although interest and support came from many countries, including some developed ones, in the end it came to naught because of differences within the industrialized West. Most of the major proposals emerging from UNCTAD have suffered a similar fate. At the same time, even when ideas are not immediately implemented they can make a difference, as Stéphane Hessel told us in connection with human rights in 1948 and the Development Decades: "It is useful to have words, even if they are not followed by deeds."

At a time, when the international pendulum has swung strongly in favor of the benefits of free trade, and when the WTO is at the center of negotiations with free trade as its ruling philosophy, it is worth emphasizing that this is far from an adequate description of how the economic world is operating at present, especially with respect to poorer countries dependent on commodity exports. The long-run tendency of the terms of trade to decline has acted—and still acts—strongly against the interests of poorer and weaker developing countries.

The reality of international trade and other economic relationships is often far from free. Unfair trade and unequal economic relationships would often be a more accurate description, with subsidies and nontariff barriers in many of the richest countries preventing free trade in agriculture and other products as well. As the Toyes make clear in their summary chapter on the future, many of the proposals on trade and finance originally formulated by UNCTAD, however unacceptable when first put forward, still have relevance. If and when the more powerful countries begin to see it in their interest for the poorer parts of the world to achieve more dynamic economies, some of these proposals are available for resuscitation.

We end this section by quoting the Toyes about why the UN in its first two decades was able to undertake unorthodox analysis with tolerance, if not enthusiastic support, from the capitalist world.

The paradox of a twenty years revolt against free trade orthodoxy by economists inside the United Nations is partially explained by two remarkable changes in the global landscape of political power that occurred during the two decades after the Second World War. One was the start of the "Cold War" between the United States and its allies and the Soviet Union and its allies, while the other was the decision of European countries to grant independent statehood to their former colonies, partly as a consequence of U.S. pressure. These two profound currents were mediated by the UN system's rule of majority voting. They created a momentum in favour of paying much more attention in international forums to the aspirations of the new leaders of poor, less-developed countries than had ever previously been paid. At the same time, the hopes placed by those leaders in the postwar international economic settlement were being severely disappointed. Marshall Plan aid was to be confined to Europe. The laboriously negotiated International Trade Organization (ITO), whose constitution reflected at least some of the trade and development concerns of the underdeveloped countries, never came into being. The General Agreement on Tariffs and Trade (GATT)—a transitional entity that came to partially substitute for the ITO—concentrated its efforts throughout the 1950s on reducing tariffs on industrial goods, an issue of limited importance to the many underdeveloped countries that had yet to industrialize (p. 5).

It may be that a future confluence of political and economic factors—linked perhaps to the need for achieving greater international stability and diminishing the widespread sense of global injustice—will bring back some of this thinking, and the proposals that went with it, to the agenda of international economic relations.

Aid and Technical Assistance

Olav Stokke's forthcoming *The UN and Development Cooperation* argues that a major date for international development assistance was December 1948, when the UN General Assembly passed resolution 198 (III) that recommended "to give further and urgent consideration to the whole problem of economic development of underdeveloped countries in *all* aspects." It passed another resolution dealing more particularly with the role of technical assistance in promoting economic development, the field in which the UN came to put strongest emphasis during the following years.

As was the case so often in those early years, the response with the greatest impact came from Washington. President Harry Truman, in his inaugural address on 20 January 1949, announced a program "for peace and freedom in four major courses of action." In point four he set out "a bold new program for making the benefits of our scientific advances and industrial progress available for the improvement and growth of underdeveloped areas" with the aim "to help the free peoples of the world, through their own efforts, to produce more food, more clothing, more material for housing, and more mechanical power to lighten their burden."[32] Other countries were invited to pool their technological resources in this undertaking.

Soon afterward, the United Nations established the Expanded Program for Technical Assistance. This international program removed the national flags, with associated strings, so characteristic of emerging bilateral aid programs. The objectives and principles set for UN assistance reflected norms that had signal effects beyond multilateral aid relations. The primary objective was to strengthen the economies of underdeveloped countries through "the development of their industries and agriculture with a view to promoting their economic and political independence in the spirit of the Charter of the United Nations."[33] The guidelines stated explicitly that assistance should be provided only at the request of the recipient government and should not infringe on its sovereignty. The assistance was to be administered on the basis of country programs to be integrated in the development plans of the countries. From the outset, a division of labor was instituted between the UN's specialized agencies and other institutions, on the one hand, and this central funding body for the world organization, on the other.

More than half a century later, similar ideas are being pursued—now with eradication of poverty as the main objective, national Poverty Reduction Strategy Papers as the major instrument, and ownership as the norm—along with policy coherence based on the priorities of the aid recipients.

It was recognized early on that economic development required not only technical assistance (or "human investment" as it came to be called), but also major additions to capital, that is physical investment. In the late 1940s and early 1950s, the UN launched an ambitious plan to provide the latter, initially under the name of the Special UN Fund for Economic Development—the "special" was added to avoid the acronym UNFED, which actually would have been a more accurate description. This fund was supposed to provide soft loans, even grants, to poor countries, with emphasis on infrastructure. There were endless discussions during the 1950s. A majority of countries favored setting up SUNFED. However, the major Western powers preferred a different arrangement for capital aid on concessionary terms outside the United Nations. In the end, a soft window was established in 1960 within the World Bank—where donor countries were at the helm—the International Development Association. The UN was left with a small kitty for pre-investment activities, and in 1965 this Special Fund merged with the Expanded Program of Technical Assistance to become the UN Development Programme.

An important proposal, supported by the Kennedy administration, resulted in the creation of the World Food Programme in 1961. And as explained earlier, the Kennedy proposal for a Development Decade led to a goal for aid, initially for total public and private transfers to underpin an acceleration of growth in developing countries, calculated to require total transfers of 1 percent of developed country national income to developing countries. In the Second Development Decade, a similar calculation led to the famous 0.7 percent target for official development assistance.

In the field of aid and technical assistance, the UN has consistently emphasized—and this is a crucial line—social development and poverty eradication. This emphasis became particularly important in the 1980s when the Washington Consensus and structural adjustment became the leading policy, orchestrated by the World Bank and IMF. The UN, initially on the defensive, stood firm and came out with important initiatives and ideas. The best known, and this has already been signaled, are "adjustment with a human face" and the *Human Development Report* series that underlined the need for a broader concept of development.

The Millennium Development Goals may be the start of a more imaginative and realistic type of development assistance. Until 2000 when they were adopted, the emphasis of development aid had largely been on input targets for growth, with the elusive 0.7 percent target as the best known. At first sight, the UN Millennium Summit that launched the MDGs seemed to have gone from one extreme to the other—from input to an exclusive focus on output targets. But that was premature. We have seen that the UN has routinely established output and input targets. Today the Millennium Project has formulated a plan that sets out an economic strategy as well as a calculation of the necessary inputs to achieve the MDGs by 2015.

And so, at the beginning of the 21st century, it looks as if development assistance is getting a second lease on life. The World Bank and IMF are on board. Specific targets have been set and inputs defined (both in policy terms and as estimates that aid must go up to 0.5 percent of GNP by 2015 to achieve the MDGs for poverty reduction). And the 0.7 percent goal for total aid has received further endorsement. World attention has been refocused. Some may think that yet another attempt to achieve big increases in development assistance is unrealistic. Distinguishing countries that are ready to productively absorb additional capital inflows and those that are not is clearly essential.

Responses to the December 2004 tsunami disaster demonstrated that many individuals in rich as well as poor countries will still respond strongly to needs for assistance—that is, there is little "fatigue" if needs are demonstrated and effective programs exist. It is now up to the United Nations and especially the rich countries to initiate the longer-term action to enable many developing countries, and especially the least developed among them, to stand on their own feet. This goes far beyond increased development assistance to include generalized trade liberalization as well as fair deals in technology and pharmaceuticals. But additional aid is an essential element.

Foreign Direct Investment and Transnational Corporations

While the Covenant of the League of Nations referred to an open and nondiscriminatory international economic environment for investment, that organization—and scholarship at the time—dealt primarily with trade. Foreign direct investment (FDI) was rarely relevant or even studied. The paucity of theory about FDI in the first half of the 20th century was proportionate to its perceived insignificance in the real world.

This changed dramatically after World War II. FDI as a policy issue gained prominence. It became a major form of international economic involvement as internationalization and decolonization combined to accelerate its flow. The rapid postwar expansion of U.S. foreign investment in Europe followed the need of European countries to rebuild their infrastructure. Scholars and policymakers were then drawn to the subject and to the entities that were its conduit: multinational corporations.

The creation of the UN provided the forum to take up foreign investment. It was now given renewed emphasis as a vehicle for economic development and as an instrument for the distribution of capital and technology in an internationalizing world. *The United Nations and Transnationals: From Code to Compact,* by Tagi Sagafi-nejad in collaboration with John Dunning, traces the ideas that the UN has launched in this highly sensitive field, examining their impact on policy, knowledge creation, and capacity building, with emphasis on developing countries. The authors begin with the establishment of the Group of Eminent Persons at the beginning of the 1970s, the UN Centre on Transnational Corporations, and the later continuation of the Centre's work by UNCTAD.

The attitude toward FDI and transnational corporations (TNCs) has changed dramatically—from critical in the 1970s to benevolent in the 1990s. The ideas of the UN on the subject have seen a parallel evolution, from confrontation and a focus on a code of conduct to cooperation and voluntary agreements. The world organization has been instrumental in bringing to the attention of the international policy arena the need for a multilateral approach to harness the activities of TNCs toward the betterment of all stakeholders. Although the centerpiece of this policy initiative, the Code of Conduct discussed during the 1970s, did not come to pass, ideas within it—on competition, pricing, marketing, resource allocation, labor relations, the environment, and corruption—survived. They resurfaced in other forums, and in a shape more compatible with the changing times. The UN once again reflects the tone of the new era through its 1999 Global Compact, which became operational in July 2000 and seeks to advance responsible corporate citizenship so that business can be part of the solution to the challenges of globalization.

A number of conventions about TNCs have been negotiated under the auspices of UN agencies. The Tripartite Declaration was negotiated through the ILO; the Framework Convention on Tobacco Control was championed by the World Health Organization; and the principles concerning restrictive business practices were discussed under UNCTAD, where bilateral investment treaties and investment promotion agencies were also given wings. These crucial ideas either emanated from, or germinated and matured within, the UN system.

Besides these codes and their approximations, other policy ideas are examined, such as the 1985 and 1989 hearings on Apartheid and FDI in South Africa, joint ventures between Western TNCs and Soviet firms that came out of the UN Centre on Transnational Corporations, and a key intellectual output—the annual *World Investment Report* published since 1991.

The overarching conclusion must be that the UN has provided a useful forum for the world and a mirror to see itself, gravitating always closer to the center as member states have sometimes swung to extremes. Through it all, the world organization has remained the spawning ground for ideas that have the potential to make foreign direct investment and transnational corporations more beneficial to humankind.

Opposing Orthodoxy

Ideas are rarely realized without a battle. From early on the UN struggled against the orthodoxy of the day. The world organization's contributions have often stood in sharp contrast to the reigning orthodoxy of the financially well-heeled World Bank and IMF. Partly this reflected the different political base of the two institutions, with the UN having equal representation of all countries and the Bretton Woods institutions a voting system weighted to reflect financial contributors.

Not surprisingly, the Bretton Woods institutions have tended to produce analyses and policy recommendations that reflected the interests and perspectives of developed countries while the UN has tended in another direction—namely analyses, ideas, and recommendations more in tune with those of developing countries that constitute the bulk of member states. James O. C. Jonah told us about this difference in perspectives: "That is why the Americans never accepted UNCTAD and others, because they think that, in contrast to the IMF and the World Bank, you don't have a weighted voting . . . Whereas the Third World was saying, 'Yes, we need equal voting.'"

Sharp differences were visible even in the 1950s. Major battles over SUNFED ensued. The UN produced a succession of reports, arguing the case for concessional funding for developing countries. The World Bank, notably its former president Eugene Black, dismissed the case and argued that such funding would be anti-market, dependent on subsidies from the industrial countries, and altogether against the interests of developing countries. Only at the end of the 1950s, after nine years of highly contentious and often tortuous debate, was the matter brought to a resolution, with a historic compromise. The UN would be allowed to have a special fund though on a much smaller scale from the original SUNFED proposal. Concessional funding would become a program of the World Bank, notwithstanding their many years of steady opposition. Thus was born IDA, which continues as the main international instrument for providing concessional assistance to the poorest countries. SUNFED is one of the many fascinating "what ifs" of the UN's intellectual history.

In the 1980s alternative approaches to adjustment became a focus of UN analysis and debate. UNICEF came up with *Adjustment with a Human Face.* The Economic Commission for Africa came out with the African Alternative Framework for Structural Adjustment Programs. Both institutions recognized the need for adjustment but both argued that the criteria used by the World Bank were too narrow and leading to ineffective programs. Evaluations by the World Bank and the IMF consistently showed that only one or two goals were being achieved—in almost all cases, those of reducing inflation and sometimes, but by no means always, closing budgetary gaps. In only a few cases was economic growth accelerating. As Gerry Helleiner told us: "The legacy of the neoliberal thrust of the 1980s will be close to zero. They moved things back in the right direction but greatly overshot. It would have been wiser and less costly to move back in a gradual fashion, rather than in the really roughhouse manner in which they did."

The neglect of health, education, nutrition, and other human needs in the framing of adjustment had serious human consequences. As UNICEF argued, if child malnutrition rose as a consequence of adjustment, there generally was no second chance. This is not only inhuman but also contrary to the economic principles and purposes of sound investment and sensible adjustment. The ILO also took up the cudgels—and in the late 1980s planned a major international conference to debate alternatives to adjustment. The United States, not pleased, threatened once again to leave the ILO if this conference proceeded. In its place, a smaller and more technical conference was organized, with only limited participation.

Although greeted initially with skepticism, UN alternatives to adjustment have over the years been increasingly accepted, at least rhetorically. Indeed by the late 1990s, the World Bank had broadened its approaches to development and is now fully committed to the pursuit of poverty reduction, the MDGs, and a broader notion of development. Its former president, James Wolfensohn, and others in the Washington-based international financial institutions seemed to have gotten "old-fashioned UN religion." Though the IMF states that it is equally committed, in practice it largely pursues its traditional agenda of adjustment, arguing that these are the conditions for long-run stability needed to underpin programs of growth and poverty reduction.

A third major area where the UN became the major dissident international voice was in the pursuit of a more gradual and institutional approach to transition, spelled out in Yves Berthelot and Paul Rayment's chapter in *Unity and Diversity in Development Ideas: Perspectives from the Regional Commissions*. The Economic Commission for Europe in 1989 and 1990 championed a path to transition problems in Central and Eastern Europe that stood in stark contrast to the pursuit of a "big bang," which became the conventional wisdom. The ECE argued that the process of transition could not be rushed, that institutional change should be planned and supported and be an early part of reform. Neglecting institutional reform, any sudden installation of market capitalism was bound to fail. It took most of a decade for this to be generally accepted.

It is wrong to suggest that the UN has always been a dissenting voice to Washington orthodoxy. On some issues, the Bretton Woods and the UN institutions have come together. Perhaps the closest was during the McNamara years when the World Bank proposed a sharp focus on poverty reduction and work toward this end was pursued by Chief Economist Hollis Chenery, who co-authored *Redistribution with Growth*.[34] Four years later, Mahbub ul Haq and Paul Streeten produced a succession of studies on basic needs, summarized in an influential volume.[35] In these cases the mutual reinforcement of UN and Bretton Woods reflected strong leadership by the World Bank president and strong professional support from key economists within the Bank, several there on short-term assignments.

Global Governance

In *Ahead of the Curve?* we wrote that "at the beginning of the 21st century a paradoxical situation has arisen . . . at the global level. An economy propelled by energetic and dynamic global enterprises is booming, while many states grow poorer . . . In many respects, a countervailing power is required for the planet . . . acting on a global scale to redefine the responsibility of states" (p. 137). The convergence of development with human security and human rights also argues for a more active role of the UN in global governance. This is the *raison d'être* behind *The UN and Global Governance: An Idea and its Prospects,* by Ramesh Thakur and Thomas G. Weiss. As this book is in its early stages, we concentrate here on definitions and approaches.

There are vast disparities in power and influence among states, international organizations, corporations, and NGOs. Since 1945 the United Nations has made continual efforts to develop and adapt better intergovernmental machinery to respond to challenges of the environment, development, human rights, and security. However, the intergovernmental institutions that collectively underpin global governance are insufficient in number, inadequately resourced, and sometimes incoherent in their separate policies and philosophies.

One of the more dramatic changes over the last 60 years is the number of actors more routinely involved in UN deliberations—not simply state authorities but also other intergovernmental secretariats, NGOs, for-profit corporations, civil society writ large, and the media. This healthy pluralization of UN affairs is bound to accelerate in the 21st century. The most widely cited definition comes from the Commission on Global Governance: "Governance is the sum of the many ways individuals and institutions, public and private, manage their common affairs."[36] Sonny Ramphal, one of the co-chairs, told us why the commission's work was crucial: "It brought together all the elements that were in need of being brought together globally . . . We weren't paying enough attention there to changing the world . . . to international governance, to the evolution from the age of the nation-state."

Thakur and Weiss define "global governance" as collective efforts to identify, understand, or address worldwide problems that go beyond the capacity of individual states to solve. Global governance—which can be good or bad, just as national governance—refers to concrete cases of cooperative problem solving. The instruments may be rules (laws, norms, codes of behavior), as well as institutions and practices to manage collective affairs by a variety of actors. Global governance thus refers to the complex of institutions, mechanisms, relationships, and processes between and among states, markets, citizens, and organizations to articulate collective interests on the global plane, establish rights and obligations, and mediate differences.

The UN and Global Governance will emphasize the diverse roles of the United Nations as an "intellectual actor" in global governance whose contributions have included identifying and diagnosing problems; developing norms; formulating recommendations; and on occasion implementing and sustaining a regime. The book will discuss the way that the world organization has or has not filled these roles within various historical cases that illustrate the gaps between global problems and global solutions.

The notion of global governance, and the details of how it works and does not, will grow in relevance with a globalizing world economy. We have shown in the preceding pages how much remains to be done in bringing more justice to bear on such problems as global income gaps, international trade, human rights, and human security. The road ahead is difficult. Thakur and Weiss will show what has already been accomplished and how to proceed, emphasizing the critical necessity to strengthen intergovernmental institutions.

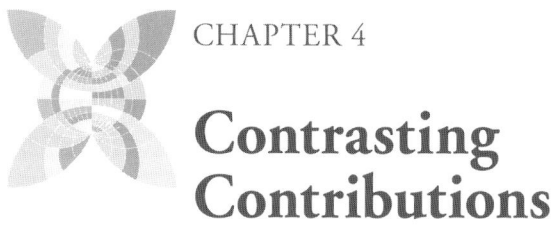

CHAPTER 4

Contrasting Contributions

Nothing in the preceding summaries should suggest monolithic views within the UN system. Indeed, the history of UN ideas over the last 60 years suggests a cornucopia of perspectives. Here we tease out two sources of the diverse inputs into analyses and policy recommendations—from the world's regions and from civil society.

Regional Perspectives

A strong point of the United Nations, almost from the very beginning, was its regional and country perspectives. This instilled a sense of the diversity and complexity of the development process, as well as giving the UN an authentic regional voice and a special sensitivity to the cultural richness of the world. As Yves Berthelot comments in the introduction to his edited volume, *Unity and Diversity in Development Ideas*: *Perspectives from the UN Regional Commissions,* "the culture specific to each may be the most distinctive contribution that the regional commissions have made to the intellectual history of the UN" (p. 7).

In creating the regional commissions, there was in every case resistance and delay. A few governments opposed their establishment in principle, noting that the Charter did not envisage such institutions and wondering whether the commissions would create regional divisions and work against efforts to build a more unified world. But the more general arguments were those endlessly repeated when international institutions propose initiatives—the risk of duplication and the fear of additional cost, voiced especially by developed countries.

This concern did not cause much hesitation when it came to the creation of the Organisation for European Economic Co-operation in 1948—which later became the Organisation for Economic Co-operation and Development (OECD)—or the creation of CEET (the unit for Eastern Europe established within OECD) in 1989. Both these institutions were established when the UN's Economic Commission for Europe was already in place and acknowledged to have the professional expertise and programs to deal with the very same issues as the proposed institutions. Moreover, the economic staff of the U.S. State Department was overruled when they suggested that for the Marshall Plan the ECE "would be the most appropriate agency for handling such a program." No less a distinguished figure than Walt W. Rostow recommended that ECE should take on these functions.

Although the success of the Marshall Plan in rebuilding Europe is obvious, an intriguing "what if?" arises. Could the same results have also occurred under UN auspices? This crucial path not taken has clear consequences for the long-run development role of the United Nations. As Berthelot comments, "had the subsequent work of the OECD been developed within the UN, not only the ECE but also ECOSOC would have been greatly strengthened" (pp. 50 and 62).

Regardless of the controversies over births, the UN's regional commissions have made many important contributions, which are well documented in *Unity and Diversity.* The ECE, founded in 1947, sustained the idea of an undivided Europe over a long period of political vicissitudes. Over its first 10 years under the distinguished leadership of Gunnar Myrdal, later a winner of the Nobel Prize in economics, the ECE constructed and maintained a bridge between Eastern and Western Europe. It provided the one forum where throughout the Cold War, representatives of East and Western Europe could meet to exchange information on economic and social issues. The ECE pioneered many regional programs, as well as issuing an annual *Economic Survey of Europe,* a model of professional and independent commentary on the whole region (pp. 51–131).

Also founded in 1947, ECAFE (Economic Commission for Asia and the Far East, later ESCAP) was promoted as "The Economic Parliament of Asia," by its first executive director, P. S. Lokanathan. It helped to foster a deep sense of the unity of the world's largest region (with a population today of about 3.5 billion). It documented and encouraged strategies and programs for development, many of which have become examples of best practice (pp. 132–67).

ECLA (later to become ECLAC, incorporating the Caribbean in its name) was founded in 1948 and led by Raúl Prebisch for the first 14 years. More than any other commission, ECLA under his leadership was a powerhouse of creative thinking. It developed a distinctive intellectual approach to development, building regional economic strategies to tackle the deep asymmetry of trade benefits in favor of developed countries through industrialization and regional cooperation. Though many of the early policies—import-substituting industrialization, structuralist approaches to inflation—have been abandoned, and rightly so, the impact on development thinking and action has been profound (pp. 168–232).

The Economic Commission for Africa was established in 1958, despite opposition from the then-colonial powers. It soon became a strong voice for regional and subregional cooperation throughout Africa, later developing the Lagos Plan of Action, a strategy for African self-reliance. In the 1980s, ECA argued strongly for an African Alternative Framework for Structural Adjustment Programs.

ECWA (Economic Commission for West Asia, later to become ESCWA by adding "social" to its remit) was established in 1973. It serves the smallest region in terms of population (about 160 million), which also is one of the most unequal in income and economic performance and the most afflicted by long-simmering conflicts and tensions. Its strong commitment to regional cooperation is reinforced by the fact that many natural obstacles to development in the Middle East and North Africa can be effectively addressed only in a regional context (pp. 307–57).

In addition to their role in regional leadership, the commissions have made other contributions to the realm of ideas and policy analysis. Trade analysis and policy has been one important economic area; but industry, energy, and transport have also been points of focus, as well as social policies in education, health, and social welfare, along with technical assistance and other programs of support. Other pioneering contributions of the regional commissions that have made a significant impact on the UN as a whole are found in the box.

Civil Society

Almost every volume in our United Nations Intellectual History Project series and the vast majority of those interviewed for the oral history highlight the crucial role in international affairs and the distinct perspectives of civil society. Of course, the Charter itself was forward-looking. It begins with the words, "We the peoples," when one might have expected an initial and resounding emphasis on "We the [Sovereignty-Bound] Member States." And Charter Article 71 specifically makes provision for the contributions from nonstates in the form of "suitable arrangement for consultation with nongovernmental organizations which are concerned with matters within its competence." Over the years, there has been a slow and dramatic growth in the role and influence by NGOs in

Selected Intellectual Contributions by Regional Commissions

Women in Development. ECA, in the early and mid-1960s, organized meetings on the role of women in community development, urban development, and national social and economic development. This was well ahead of other commissions and long before the central importance of women in economic development was realized, including by the UN as a whole. Later, ESCWA skillfully stepped into the sensitive minefield of Middle East debate relating to women, population, labor conditions, and migration, raising essential questions from within the region and avoiding the explosions that might have arisen had they been raised from outside.

Development Planning. The regional commissions played a central role in support of national planning, especially from the 1950s to 1970s. The Marshall Plan had already made national planning an essential condition for receiving U.S. support. Planning was in vogue at the time, and all regional commissions gave attention to it, often with the World Bank providing advice and support to countries. The approach was generally that of "indicative planning," not the centralized state version à la USSR. The emphasis was on clarifying national objectives and goals, achieving coherence between objectives and policy instruments, and pursuing institutional change and proper sequencing—all issues that could not be left entirely to market forces. Although by the mid-1970s the vogue of planning was in decline, economic progress in all regions over the 1960s and 1970s was substantially greater than in the 1980s and 1990s, except for China.

Regionalization versus Globalization. Given the publicity accorded to the global village and global markets, ECE, ECLAC, and ESCAP have underlined the under-emphasized fact that trade within their regions has grown more rapidly than it has globally. This indicates a much closer integration of the countries within their region than toward a more global engagement.

Independent Regional Analyses. A final pioneering contribution was the production of regional surveys. In the cases of the ECE and ECLAC, they helped launch an institutional independent commentary free from political interference. Gunnar Myrdal's comments have a general resonance: "There are few things in my life I feel so proud of as having had a role in building up and defending this tradition of independent truth-seeking in an international secretariat" (p. 65).

UN corridors and elsewhere. Viru Dayal, the *chef de cabinet* for two secretaries-general, told us: "I think that the work of the world—if that doesn't sound too pompous—can only benefit from the involvement of civil society . . . Besides, civil society knows where the shoe pinches. They know when to laugh and they know when to cry."

The sheer growth in NGO numbers over the UN's lifetime has been nothing short of remarkable, both of international as well as national ones. Whatever the ideas under discussion—human rights or gender, children or minority groups, the environment or development aid—the voices coming from outside of governments have been essential to the quality of the conversation within the UN and the global conferences. They have often made decisive contributions ensuring that governments themselves took action.

NGOs and other looser associations of what increasingly is called "global civil society" are thus inserting themselves into a wide range of intergovernmental deliberations. They occupy spheres of ideas, values, institutions, organizations, networks, and individuals somewhere between the family, the state, and the market. The state system that has governed the world for centuries is unlikely to disappear any time soon. However, the presence of alternative voices has become an integral part of the UN system's processes of deliberations and of world politics more generally, what some would call, including some of us, the "third UN."

The role of civil society has been important in all areas of UN activity. But it has been most crucial in the case of women and children, the environment, and human rights, as underlined in our volumes on these topics. The Global Compact has been instrumental in getting business more closely interested and involved in UN activities. In recalling her involvement in NGOs before assuming the helm at UNIFEM, Noeleen Heyzer told us about the challenges of pushing out the envelope on women's issues: "At one stage, there was a big divide between research and activism, and I wanted to bridge that gap. I felt that it was important to have very solid analysis to influence activism. Activism without knowledge and without analysis can go astray. But at the same time, research without the kind of activism and commitment that I saw on the ground could not bring about the transformation needed to improve the lives of people marginalized by development."

These developments have not occurred without criticism, often from the very civil society that was brought on board. The degree to which NGOs are accountable and representative has been an issue—"loose cannons" to many observers. Having private enterprise get closer to the UN is "a double-edged sword" to many. But those interested in ideas cannot ignore these voices, often at piercing decibel levels, coming from outside governments.

CHAPTER 5

Omissions, Distortions, and Failures

Even with all the pioneering work and intellectual leadership, our investigation of the UN's historical record also reveals important gaps—in either conception or execution.[37] Over the years, important ideas were sometimes floated, then forgotten. Perhaps more common were ideas created—but then dropped, distorted, even consciously destroyed, reinterpreted, or absorbed into a quite different frame.

The United Nations Intellectual History Project has identified issues and challenges that have not been met or that have been diverted, leading to missed opportunities. We shall mention only a few, all of which figure in several of the UNIHP's volumes.

Slow Reaction to the Washington Consensus

Why did we have to wait until the 1990s to get some kind of a coherent alternative to the Washington Consensus? It had strengths: strong theoretical foundations, clear policy implications for a wide range of economic and financial issues, strong support from powerful countries. But there were and remain important gaps and omissions mostly neglected by the neoliberal paradigm. Examples are the noneconomic issues and other concerns beyond the market such as intrahousehold income distribution, gender inequalities, and the human concerns of the aged and of young children. In short, any alternative must be more microeconomic and social, must include many more noneconomic variables, and must concentrate on human values.

As ILO Director General Juan Somavia told us: "We still haven't been able to get to the point where the powers that be will actually acknowledge that a mere combination of privatization, deregulation, and the reduction of the role of the state is not going to produce the solutions." The human development paradigm meets these requirements. However, its application in practice requires theoretical strength and intellectual courage—two requirements that are not always in abundant supply within the UN.

Global Gaps in Income and Wealth

Issues of global inequality were seen as central in the early economic work of the United Nations, rising to a major point of debate and policy concern with the call for a new international economic order in the mid-1970s. Following the stalemate over this debate and the removal of the New International Economic Order from the international agenda, issues of global inequality became marginalized. In the last few years, however, they have been creeping back. Inequality is being "brought in from the cold,"[38] with both UN and the Bretton Woods institutions according it more attention.

Although there is disagreement about the meaning and size of the global income gap, there is no doubt that the per capita income differences between the richest and poorest countries have increased. The same is true of the chasm between the income of the poorest and richest 10 percent of the world's population. Such inequalities have deep implications for global governance and the functioning of the world economy, as well as for human welfare and global equity. Policy ideas are urgently required, and future UN research and analysis need to return more systematically to this topic.

Debt Relief

Over the years, the UN has analyzed the external debt of developing countries and formulated many proposals for action. In the 1987 *Trade and Development Report*, for example, UNCTAD identified the weaknesses of the international debt strategy pursued in the 1980s, emphasizing "the failure to conceive it within a broader strategy for accelerating growth in the world economy." The report added: "rapidly expanding export earnings are fundamental to any successful debt strategy and, without them, the objectives of accelerating growth in debtor countries and achieving financial viability cannot be reconciled."[39]

Despite this analysis and many subsequent proposals for action, it took another 10 years to develop the heavily indebted poor country (HIPC) program. It then took several more years to agree that this version of the program was inadequate and to introduce modifications to improve it.

To be fair, the World Bank's former chief economist, Joseph Stiglitz, candidly acknowledged that many in the World Bank recognized by

1989 that "growth in the debtor countries would not return without debt relief . . . but . . . none of them could openly confront the existing strategy without having an alternative to put in place. And . . . so long as the United States was not willing to move, the IFIs [international financial institutions] were not free to speak."[40]

Digging by the Toyes for *The UN and Global Political Economy* made clear that, in the words of the U.K.'s chancellor of the exchequer Nigel Lawson from 1983–89, "[T]he principal—though largely undeclared—objective of the Western world's debt strategy, ably coordinated by the IMF, was to buy time . . . Time was needed not only to enable the debtor countries to put sensible economic policies in place but also for the Western banks to rebuild their shattered balance sheets to the point where they could afford to write off their bad sovereign debts. For it was perfectly clear that the vast bulk of these debts would never come good—even though there was an understandable conspiracy of silence over admitting this unpalatable fact" (p. 260).

One must conclude that the HIPC program, even in its latest version, is grossly inadequate: too little, too late, and with only a handful of countries where it appears to be truly succeeding. That is the sad result over two decades of having ignored or distorted UN ideas and proposals.

Special Measures for the Least Developed Countries and for Africa

As early as 1964 UNCTAD at its founding conference identified the need for special attention to "the less developed among the developing countries." Four years later a resolution was passed on the needs of the least developed countries. In 1971, 24 countries were identified and placed on the original list. By 1998 the number of least developed countries had grown to 49, accounting for some 10 percent of the world's people with a population of more than 600 million. This growth in their population and membership is a tragic reminder of the collective failure to deal with the most marginalized countries.

By the late 1970s it was clear that many of these countries lagged seriously behind in development. UNCTAD organized a major conference on the least developed countries in 1981. As these countries continued to fall ever further behind, subsequent conferences were held in 1990 and 2001, producing specific ideas and targets, such as setting aside 0.15 percent of GNP in development aid for them. Although the UN has led the way in identifying many specific actions to accelerate growth and development in these countries, international support has egregiously fallen short of agreed goals. Nor has the World Bank or the IMF formally recognized the least developed category of countries. The failures of the world community to respond to the clearly identified needs of these countries must be judged more than 20 years later to be one of the most serious omissions of action for development.

The developing region with the bulk of least developed countries is Africa. As the Economic Commission for Africa underscored: "The contrast between the lives led by those who live in rich countries and poor people in Africa is the greatest scandal of our age."[41] Substantial intellectual energy has gone into examining the continent's problems and prospects. The New Partnership for Africa's Development (NEPAD) is one illustration, and the Millennium Project another. The numerous attempts to shake up the G-7 into launching a Marshall Plan for Africa are to be commended as an indication of the scale of action required, even if so far the donor world has not been willing.

HIV/AIDS

In preparation for the Millennium Summit in September 2000, the Secretary-General put forth his vision in *"We the Peoples": The Role of the United Nations in the 21st Century.*[42] This set out the challenges of improving international governance in the emerging global economy, identifying priorities of sustainable growth, poverty reduction, employment generation, combating HIV/AIDS, upgrading slums, and bridging the digital divide—in short, building structures for global equity and greater solidarity. On combating HIV/AIDS the UN arrived late on the scene. Despite some promising beginnings in the WHO and elsewhere, intellectual and operational action fell dramatically short of the challenge.

Other Areas

The UNIHP has unearthed other fundamental areas for action. The first is the need for rethinking what development really means. The shift of thinking to put human rights and human development at the center of the world organization's work is significant. But it does not herald the arrival at nirvana, beyond which there is nothing more to be achieved. Instead, we should continually expect new problems and new levels of awareness of human needs, possibilities, and ambitions. These will define new objectives for social, economic, and cultural development—nationally, regionally, and internationally. Further research and analytical work is expected. But it will move us ahead only if it leads to lively interaction—within universal UN and smaller intergovernmental forums. The notion that certain perspectives are anathema and should not be discussed is short-sighted, to say the least. What is politically incorrect or correct is almost always a value judgment subject to shifts in fashion, not an intellectually valid argument. Investigation has to proceed to logical ends, whatever the political consequences.

This raises a second need—for more work on culture, one of the neglected aspects of the UN's work so far, although UNESCO made a limited effort by twice issuing the *World Culture Report* (in 1998 and 2000) before halting them. Sensitivity to the diversity of cultures and traditions, and their place in the dynamics of development, will require much rethinking of conventional analysis. Globalization—both as an end and as a process—should be subjected to fundamental rethinking. Incorporating the perspectives and reactions from many regions of the world is an obvious starting point. This is not a recipe for imagining a return to some mythical past. It does suggest, however, that the trajectory for the global future cannot be taken as a simple extrapolation to all the world of the dominant consumer life styles of the developed countries or of the richer sections of the population of the developing countries.

The issues are well captured by Lourdes Arizpe, formerly a UNESCO assistant secretary-general responsible for the two editions of the *World Culture Report:* "The first challenge of the United Nations is to create a new scheme for the coexistence of different cultures that are no longer juxtaposed as a mosaic of cultures, but as currents in a single river . . . to create the spaces, identify the people who would be able to develop these concepts and perspectives, and put them in positions where they can lead this world debate on how different cultures and religions can coexist."

CHAPTER 6

The UN's Intellectual Challenges Today

We have argued that the UNIHP is about "forward-looking history." In thinking about the future, our reading of the project's findings leads us to identify briefly three types of challenges: intellectual, participatory, and personnel.

First, there are numerous areas where new thinking and research are urgently required and where the UN should be encouraged to do far more creative work. Our priority list for intellectual inquiry would include:

- The growing divide between the Islamic world and the West—with attention to the political, cultural, religious, and development dimensions.
- Measures of human security, for which integrated approaches toward comprehensive collective security should be explored beyond the traditional compass of either the military or national security forces.
- New measures to support the least developed countries and countries in transition.
- Sensitivity and action to take into account cultural aspects in the development equation, leading to regional differentiation of economic and social strategies.
- Measures to respond to the long-run challenges of environment and sustainability, where action is missing or inadequate, including global warming and measures to offset its consequences, especially for poorer countries.
- Global economic inequalities—once front and center—should return to the agenda, along with international measures to moderate and diminish those inequalities and their consequences.

- Mechanisms to ensure genuine international competition and free markets, with especial attention to operations of transnational corporations.

Second, actions are needed in the longer run to strengthen developing country participation in the management of the global economy. The other side of this coin is to offset the imbalances in bargaining power facing weaker countries when participating in global economic institutions. Our examination of UN history has revealed how asymmetrical power among countries has shaped global economic relationships and institutional structures. One of the major contributions of the world organization has been to analyze the implications for the economic and social development of poorer countries and to devise possible corrective measures. As we move further into the 21st century, faster progress toward the Millennium Development Goals in the poorest and least developed countries is necessary but not enough. More direct measures are also necessary to strengthen and make more effective the participation of these countries in global economic dialogue. These include:

- Recognizing formally the problems caused by asymmetries of economic power and the factors underlying them.
- Devising measures to offset these asymmetries. Examples are the appointment of groups of experts to support weaker countries, or the provision of independent assessments of proposed agreements (especially in trade, debt relief, and technology transfer) and the establishment of mechanisms of appeal, such as the appointment of an ombudsman in key international economic institutions. More public acknowledgement of these issues and more publicity for the implications of agreements under negotiation would also be useful.
- Requesting the appropriate UN institutions to work with the WTO and the Bretton Woods institutions on these issues and to report regularly on progress to diminish extreme asymmetries of bargaining power and economic participation.

Third, on the occasion of the 60th anniversary, the priority challenges ahead in economic and social development require the United Nations to seize its comparative advantage—by returning to intellectual leadership. This means strengthening the institutional capacity to generate and disseminate original ideas—in short, to ensure creative thinking.

Important proposals for UN reform are already on the table. But the mere mention of "reform" tends to make the eyes glaze over. One way to restore vitality is to infuse the neglected and vital intellectual dimension. Specific measures are required to strengthen this aspect in the immediate future. Concrete examples emerging from the United Nations Intellectual History Project include five steps. These are all "Track II" reforms that do not require constitutional changes (that is, official approval by member states) or additional resources. They will, however, require vision, courage, and leadership:

- The recognition by all parts of the UN system that contributions to ideas, thinking, analysis, and monitoring should be a major part of their work.
- To this end, the UN needs to foster an environment that encourages and rewards creative thinking of the highest intellectual

Bringing Together UN and Bretton Woods Institutions

Since 1980 the donor community has channeled growing resources to the Bretton Woods institutions and increasingly followed their lead in policy and action, both internationally and at the country level. For coordination and policy coherence, this has meant a positive advance over the anarchy and donor competition of earlier years. But it has come at a price. The overwhelming focus on the international financial institutions has frequently led to neglect of UN organizations, leaving them marginalized in influence and advice, with their capacity to fulfill earlier roles diminished because of severely reduced funds.

Our assessment of the record shows the many respects in which this pattern has been counterproductive. UN contributions have been neglected in key areas where the Bretton Woods institutions were not active or, equally important, where subsequent events have shown that their earlier policies either were wrong or narrow. A better balance is required between the World Bank, the IMF, and the United Nations—in policy leadership as well as in funding and support for national and international actions. Stronger roles for the regional development banks and the regional commissions should be part of new initiatives.

The recent past provides some cause for optimism. Important changes have begun, many related to the adoption of the Millennium Development Goals in 2000 and of the Poverty Reduction Strategy Papers at the country level. The Bretton Woods institutions, the donor community, and the world organization are cooperating better within counties. Although this is an important step forward, too often UN agencies lack the resources and capacity to make the desired and feasible contribution to the partnership. UNDP, UNICEF, and the World Food Programme have a strong presence and capacity at the country level, but other members of the UN system often lack such a presence.

quality. This has implications for recruitment and promotion—to assemble under one roof, professionals from different disciplines and from different national and cultural backgrounds. The quality of staff is essential, and there can be no compromise in ensuring the highest standards of competence.

- The mobilization of more financial support for research, analysis, and policy exploration is a top priority. The terms for providing such resources are of special importance—to ensure longer term availability and flexibility and, more important, to guarantee intellectual autonomy.

- Strengthening the means to disseminate new ideas is equally important. UN outreach with a core of key reports is sometimes impressive. But too many reports languish on book shelves, coffee tables, or filing cabinets. Discussion should take place not only in intergovernmental settings but also with governments and among such diverse constituencies as business, the media, and members of civil society.

- A crucial intellectual challenge is improving relations between the UN and the Bretton Woods institutions to encourage exchanges of ideas and experience and a better balance in the allocation of international resources between them (see the box).

Previous efforts at reform have concentrated almost exclusively on the UN's political, security, and humanitarian dimensions. This concentration has now been broadened to the economic and social as well. The three reports before member states at the September 2005 summit may also change the way that the world organization pursues intellectual efforts.

Four years after the publication of the UNIHP's first book, we can assert even more fervently our 2001 conclusion: "Ideas matter. People matter." Indeed, our evaluation of the first six decades of UN history demonstrates that there have been many solid ideas and many skilled people. There could and should be more of both. They are, in our view, at the heart of the world organization's most important contributions and its comparative advantage.

Sir Richard Jolly

32, Southover High Street, Lewes, Sussex, BN7 1HX, UK

Tel: 01273 473 499 Fax: 01273 488 016

email: r.jolly@ids.ac.uk

Prof Adam Roberts
Balliol College
OXFORD
OX1

6th June 2005

Dear Adam

I am enclosing a copy of The Power of UN Ideas, which was launched last Wednesday in New York at a meeting attended also by the Secretary-General. I hope you find it useful. In my remarks I referred to The Power of Ideas as the book behind the movie – and UN Voices – The Struggle for Development and Social Justice as the movie. The latter is a full length book containing excerpts of the 73 interviews we conducted of senior people in the UN who had contributed to its economic and social work. When I get some more copies, I will be sending you a copy of UN Voices, since it has a lot of good material which I think you will enjoy.

Best wishes and thanks again for inviting me to the meeting on UN reform.

Richard

RICHARD JOLLY

M. June 05

With thanks by letter

Notes

1. High-level Panel on Threats, Challenges and Change, *A More Secure World: Our Shared Responsibility* (New York: United Nations, 2004); Millennium Project, *Investing in Development: A Practical Plan to Achieve the Millennium Development Goals* (New York: United Nations Development Programme, 2005); and Kofi A. Annan, *In Larger Freedom: Towards Development, Secuirty and Human Rights for All*, UN document A/59/2005, 21 March 2005.

2. All oral history quotes are found in Thomas G. Weiss, Tatiana Carayannis, Louis Emmerij, and Richard Jolly, *UN Voices: The Struggle for Development and Social Justice* (Bloomington: Indiana University Press, 2005) as well as in the UN Intellectual History Project's transcripts.

3. "United Nations Millennium Declaration," General Assembly resolution A/RES/55/2, 8 September 2000.

4. United Nations, *National and International Measures for Full Employment* (New York: United Nations, 1949); *Measures for the Economic Development of Under-developed Countries* (New York: United Nations, 1951); and *Measures for International Economic Stability* (New York: United Nations, 1951).

5. "Speech of 25 September 1961," reproduced in *Public Papers of the President of the United States, J.F. Kennedy, 20 January to 31 December 1961* (Washington, DC: U.S. Government Printing Office, 1962), p. 623.

6. United Nations, *The United Nations Development Decade: Proposals for Action* (New York: United Nations, 1962), pp. 10–11.

7. ILO, *Employment, Incomes and Equality: A Strategy for Increasing Productive Employment in Kenya* (Geneva: ILO, 1972).

8. Giovanni Cornia, Richard Jolly, and Frances Stewart, eds., *Adjustment with a Human Face* (Oxford: Oxford University Press, 1987), two volumes.

9. "African Alternative Framework to Structural Adjustment Programmes for Socio-Economic Recovery and Transformation," General Assembly resolution 44/49, 17 November 1989.

10. Boutros Boutros-Ghali, *An Agenda for Peace: Preventive Diplomacy, Peacemaking and Peace-keeping*, (New York: United Nations, 1992).

11.   See Kofi A. Annan, *The Question of Intervention: Speeches by the Secretary-General* (New York: United Nations, 1999); International Commission on Intervention and State Sovereignty, *The Responsibility to Protect* (Ottawa: International Development Research Centre, 2001); and Thomas G. Weiss and Don Hubert, *The Responsibility to Protect: Research, Bibliography, and Background* (Ottawa: International Development Research Centre, 2001).

12.   Boutros Boutros-Ghali, *An Agenda for Development* (New York: United Nations, 1995).

13.   Eleanor Roosevelt, "Opening Statement to the Third Session of the Third Committee," 89th Meeting GAOR, p. 32.

14.   J.P. Humphrey, *Human Rights and the United Nations: a Great Adventure,* (Dobbs Ferry, New York: International Publishers, 1984), pp. 39–40.

15.   UNDP, *Human Development Report 2000: Human Rights and Human Development* (New York: Oxford University Press, 2000).

16.   World Commission on Environment and Development, *Our Common Future* (Oxford: Oxford University Press, 1987).

17.   United Nations, *Declaration on Permanent Sovereignty over Natural Resources,* General Assembly resolution 1803 (XVII), 14 December 1962.

18.   United Nations, *United Nations Convention on the Law of the Sea,* Montego Bay, 10 December 1982 and *Supplementary Agreement,* New York, 1994. Entry into force: 16 November 1994.

19.   United Nations, *Problems of the Human Environment: Report of the Secretary-General* (New York: United Nations, 1969), p. 4.

20.   Donella H. Meadows, Jørgen Randers, and Dennis Meadows, *The Limits to Growth: A Report to the Club of Rome's Project on the Predicament of Mankind* (London: Pan, 1972).

21.   United Nations, *World Charter for Nature* (New York: United Nations, 1982).

22.   United Nations, *The Determinants and Consequences of Population Trends* (New York: United Nations, 1953).

23.   Hilkka Pietilä, "Engendering the Global Agenda: The Story of the Women and the United Nations," *Development Dossier*, United Nations Non-Governmental Liaison Service, 2002, p. 9.

24.   Irene Tinker, ed., *Persistent Inequalities: Women and World Development.* (New York: Oxford University Press, 1990), p. 20.

25.   UN Economic Commission for Africa, *Status and Role of Women in East Africa* (Addis Ababa, E/CN.14/SWSA/6, 1967), cited in Margaret C. Snyder and Mary Tadesse, *African Women and Development: A History* (Johannesburg: Witwaterstrand University Press, 1995), p. 31.

26.   Amartya Sen, *Development as Freedom* (Oxford: Oxford University Press, 1999).

27.   For the latest data and definitions, see *Human Development Report 2004: Cultural Liberty in Today's Diverse World* (Oxford: Oxford University Press, 2004), pp. 127–51.

28. United Nations, *The United Nations Development Decade: Proposals for Action* (New York: United Nations, 1962), pp. 12–13, drawing on a 1962 report "The Economic and Social Consequences of Disarmament."

29. United Nations, *The Relationship between Disarmament and Development: Report of the Secretary-General* (New York: United Nations, 1982), p. 235.

30. Devesh Kapur, John P. Lewis, and Richard Webb, eds., *The World Bank: Its First Half Century* (Washington, DC: Brookings 1997), p. 533.

31. UNDP, *Human Development Report 1994* (Oxford: Oxford University Press, 1994), p. 3.

32. Harry S. Truman, inaugural address, 20 January 1949, in *Public Papers of the Presidents, Harry S. Truman, 1949* (Washington, DC, 1964), pp. 114–15.

33. Expanded Programme of Technical Assistance for Economic Development of Under-developed Countries, *ESOSOC 222 (IX) Economic development of Under-developed Countries Resolutions*, 15 August 1949. Available at www.undp.org/bdp/pm/docs/reference-centre/chapter1/ecores222.pdf.

34. Hollis Chenery, Montek S. Ahluwalia, C. L. G. Bell, John H. Duloy, and Richard Jolly, *Redistribution with Growth: Policies to Improve Income Distribution in Developing Countries in the Context of Economic Growth* (London: Oxford University Press, 1974).

35. Paul Streeten with Shahid Javed Burki, Mahbub ul Haq, Norman Hicks, and Frances Stewart, *First Things First: Meeting Basic Human Needs in the Developing Countries* (New York: Oxford University Press, 1981).

36. Commission on Global Governance, *Our Global Neighbourhood* (Oxford: Oxford University Press, 1995), p. 2.

37. Another research project is mapping some distortions. See Morten Boas and Desmond McNeill, *Global Institutions and Development: Framing the World?* (London: Routledge, 2004).

38. In the words of A. B. Atkinson, in his presidential address to the Royal Economic Society, "Bringing Income Distribution in from the Cold," *Economic Journal* 107, issue 441 (1997), pp. 297–321.

39. UN Conference on Trade and Development, *Trade and Development Report* (Geneva: UNCTAD, 1987), p. 59.

40. I. Diwan and I. Husain, *Dealing with the Debt Crisis.* (Washington, DC: World Bank, 1989), p. v, cited in Beatriz Armendariz and Francisco Ferreira, "The World Bank and the Analysis of the International Debt Crisis," in John Harriss, Janet Hunter, and Colin M. Lewis, eds., *The New Institutional Economics and Third Development* (London: Routledge, 1995), pp. 215–29.

41. Commission for Africa, *Our Common Interest* (London: Commission for Africa, 2005), p. 22.

42. Kofi A. Annan, *"We the Peoples": The Role of the United Nations in the 21st Century* (New York: UN, 2000).